Contents

Introduction **4-5**

Homework diary **6**

Homework

Homework: Counting, partitioning and calculating
Teachers' notes **7-8**
Homework sheets **9-20**

Homework: Securing number facts, understanding shape
Teachers' notes **21-22**
Homework sheets **23-40**

Homework: Handling data and measures
Teachers' notes **41-42**
Homework sheets **43-54**

Homework: Calculating, measuring and understanding shape
Teachers' notes **55-56**
Homework sheets **57-68**

Homework: Securing number facts, relationships and calculating
Teachers' notes **69-70**
Homework sheets **71-88**

Puzzles and problems

Objectives grid **89**
Activities **90-107**

Answers

Homework answers **108-109**
Puzzles and problems answers **110-111**

About the series

100 Maths Homework Activities offers a complete solution to your planning and resourcing for maths homework activities. There are six books in the series, one for each year group from Year 1 to Year 6.

Each *100 Maths Homework Activities* book contains 72 homework activities, which cover the Renewed Framework objectives, and 36 puzzles and problems, which focus on the Using and applying objectives.

About the homework activities

Each homework activity is presented as a photocopiable page, with some supporting notes for parents and carers provided underneath the activity.

Teachers' notes relating to the activities appear in grid format at the beginning of each block's activities. When exactly the homework is set and followed up is left to your professional judgement.

Across the *100 Maths Homework Activities* series, the homework activities cover a range of homework types. Some of the activities are for sharing. These encourage the child to discuss the homework task with a parent or carer, and may, for example, involve the home context, or a game to be played with the carer. Other activities involve investigations or problem-solving tasks. Again, the parent or carer is encouraged to participate in the activity, offering support to the child, and discussing the activity and its outcomes with the child.

Unit B2 ◻ Homework activity

Name _____ Date _____

Shopping

■ Pretend you have 10p to spend.

■ Choose what you would like to buy.

1p
6p
4p
9p
5p
3p
2p
7p
8p
10p

BLOCK B

■ Will you have any change? ▢   How much? ▢

■ Now buy some different things with 10p.

Dear Helper
This activity helps your child to use their problem-solving skills. Discuss with them which things they would like to buy. They may find it helpful to 'pay' you for the items with real coins, so that they can use the coins to work out the total and find the change. Challenge your child to make several different choices of items costing up to 10p, and then to make choices with a spending limit of 20p.

◼SCHOLASTIC **PHOTOCOPIABLE**   100 MATHS HOMEWORK ACTIVITIES · YEAR 1 ◻ 29

Using the homework activities

Each homework page includes a 'Helper note', which explains the aim of the homework and how the adult can support their child if he or she cannot get started. It is recommended that some form of homework diary be used alongside these activities, through which to establish an effective home-school dialogue about the children's enjoyment and understanding of the homework. A homework diary page is provided on page 6 of this book.

Teachers' notes

The teachers' notes appear in a grid format at the start of each block's homework activities. Each grid contains the following information:

- the Framework unit
- the homework activity's title
- a brief description of the format and content of the activity, which will help you to decide which homework activity to choose
- the Renewed Framework learning objective/s
- a 'Managing the homework' section which provides two types of help – 'before' and 'after'. The 'before' notes provide suggestions for ways to introduce and explain the homework before the children take it home. These notes might include a brief oral activity to undertake as preparation for the homework. The 'after' notes provide suggestions for how to manage the review of the homework when the children return with it to school. Suggestions include discussing strategies used for solving a problem, comparing solutions, and playing a game as a class.

◼**SCHOLASTIC**

About the puzzles and problems

The puzzles and problems (pages 90-107) provide coverage of the Using and applying mathematics objectives and can be used very flexibly to provide children with a comprehensive range of fun maths tasks to take home. The grid displayed on page 89 shows which puzzles and problems cover each of the Using and applying objectives.

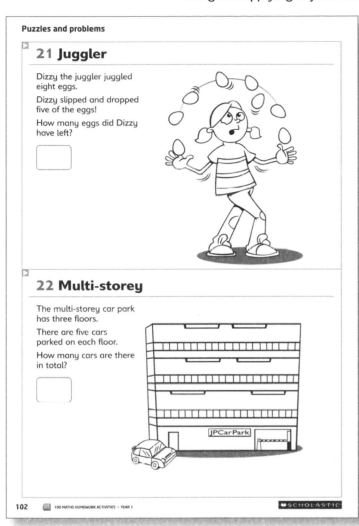

Puzzles and problems

▷ **21 Juggler**

Dizzy the juggler juggled eight eggs.

Dizzy slipped and dropped five of the eggs!

How many eggs did Dizzy have left?

▷ **22 Multi-storey**

The multi-storey car park has three floors.

There are five cars parked on each floor.

How many cars are there in total?

JPCarPark

102   ◻ 100 MATHS HOMEWORK ACTIVITIES · YEAR 1   ◼SCHOLASTIC

The puzzles and problems are based on work that the children will be covering during the year and should test their skills at that level. Some of the questions may be solved quickly, others will require more thought. Either way, children should be encouraged to try a variety of different approaches to solving problems and to look for clues and patterns in maths. It is essential for them to read the question carefully (sometimes more than once) to understand exactly what they are being asked to do. A few of the puzzles and problems will require an everyday household item or the help of a family member. Most should be readily solved by a child working on their own.

Remind the children that if a problem or puzzle is proving too difficult or frustrating, they could leave it and come back to it later with a refreshed mind!

Developing a homework policy

The homework activities have been written with the DCSF 'Homework guidelines' in mind. These can be located in detail on the Standards website **www.standards.dfes.gov. uk/homework/goodpractice** The guidelines are a good starting point for planning an effective homework policy. Effective home-school partnerships are also vital in ensuring a successful homework policy.

Encouraging home-school links

An effective working partnership between teachers and parents and carers makes a positive impact upon children's attainment in mathematics. The homework activities in this book are part of that partnership. Parents and carers are given guidance on what the homework is about, and on how to be involved with the activity. There are suggestions for helping the children who are struggling with a particular concept, such as ways of counting on or back mentally, and extension ideas for children who would benefit from slightly more advanced work.

The homework that is set across the curriculum areas for Year 1 should amount to a total of about one hour per week. The homework diary page, which can be sent home with the homework activity with opportunities for a response from the parents/carers, can be found on page 6 of this book.

Using the activities with *100 Maths Framework Lessons Year 1*

The activities covered in this book fit the planning within the book *100 Maths Framework Lessons Year 1* (also published by Scholastic Ltd). As teachers plan their work on a week-by-week basis, so the homework activities can be chosen to fit the appropriate unit of work.

Name of activity & date sent home	Child's comments		Helper's comments	Teacher's comments
	Did you like this activity? Draw a face. a lot a little not much	How much did you learn? Draw a face. a lot a little not much		

Counting, partitioning and calculating

Activity	Learning objectives	Managing the homework
A1		
Count it away Count toys with Helper as they are put away.	Count reliably at least 20 objects, recognising that when rearranged the number of objects stays the same.	**Before:** Explain that the activity will help the children to count how many there are. **After:** Encourage the children to count classroom resources as they put them away at the end of the lesson.
Fishing Child adds to make given totals. Helper encourages mental calculation.	• Relate addition to counting on; recognise that addition can be done in any order; use practical and informal written methods to support the addition of a one-digit number to a one-digit number. • Use the vocabulary related to addition and symbols to describe and record addition number sentences.	**Before:** Ask some addition questions, encouraging the children to count on in ones from the larger number. **After:** Review the homework together. Ask the children to explain how they worked out their answers.
Number search With Helper, look out for examples of numerals from 10 to 20 on the way home. Draw where these were seen and write the numbers.	Read and write numerals from 0 to 20.	**Before:** Explain that this homework will help the children to read and write numbers with more confidence. **After:** Review the homework as a class, asking individuals to write the numbers they found on the board.
Star sums Use a grid to generate sums. Work them out.	• Relate addition to counting on; recognise that addition can be done in any order; use practical and informal written methods to support the addition of a one-digit number to a one-digit number. • Use the vocabulary related to addition and symbols to describe and record addition number sentences.	**Before:** Explain that this homework will help the children to recall addition facts with numbers up to 5. **After:** Invite various children to write one of their sums on the board for the others to try.
A2		
Number snap Child and Helper play Snap with cards cut from the sheet. The cards represent numbers in different ways: cubes; numerals; abacus.	Read numerals from 0 to 20.	**Before:** Explain that the activity will help the children to recognise tens and units numbers. **After:** The game can be played in school with a partner.
Creepy crawly add Count how many in each set, then find pairs to make given totals.	• Relate addition to counting on; recognise that addition can be done in any order; use practical and informal written methods to support the addition of a one-digit number to a one-digit number. • Describe ways of solving puzzles and problems, explaining choices and decisions orally or using pictures.	**Before:** Explain that the children will need to count how many there are in each set before completing the addition sums. **After:** Mark the homework together. Ask the children to explain how they worked out the answers.
How many do you think? Estimate the number of minibeasts seen in a picture, then check by counting.	Count reliably at least 20 objects; estimate a number of objects that can be checked by counting.	**Before:** Remind the children that an estimate is a good guess of a number or amount. **After:** Using an A3 copy of the sheet, encourage the children to explain how they made their estimates.

Counting, partitioning and calculating

Activity	Learning objectives	Managing the homework
A2		
Difference of 4 Find pairs of numbers with a difference of 4.	● Understand subtraction as find a 'difference' by counting up; use practical and informal written methods to support the subtraction of a one-digit number from a one-digit or two-digit number. ● Use the vocabulary related to subtraction and symbols to describe and record subtraction number sentences.	**Before:** Ask the children to suggest a strategy for finding the difference between two numbers. **After:** Invite various children to write a 'difference of 4' number statement such as 9 − 4 = ? on the board for others to solve.
A3		
A penny more, a penny less Using 1p coins, work out how much 1p more or less than a given amount would be.	Say the number that is one more or less than any given number.	**Before:** Remind the children of strategies they can use, such as counting on or back in ones from the given number. Prepare a number track to at least 10 on the board to highlight these strategies. **After:** Ask the children some 1 more/less and 10 more/less questions. Ask them to describe the strategies they used to work these out.
More than 10 Choose pairs of numbers to make a total greater than 10. Write the addition sentences.	● Relate addition to counting on; recognise that addition can be done in any order; use practical and informal written methods to support the addition of a one-digit number to a one-digit number. ● Use the vocabulary related to addition and symbols to describe and record addition number sentences.	**Before:** Review the addition strategy of bridging through 10 (for example, 7 + 5 = 7 + 3 + 2 = 10 + 2 = 12). **After:** Invite some children to write up one of their addition sentences. Ask the others to solve it mentally. Ask them how they did it and ask the rest of the class for alternative methods of working out each answer.
Number order With Helper, play a card game that involves ordering numbers.	Compare and order numbers, using the related vocabulary.	**Before:** Ask questions about number order, such as: *Which numbers are more than ___? Which numbers are less than ___? Which numbers are between ___ and ___? Which is the next number in the sequence...? Which number is half way between ___ and ___?* **After:** Write some numbers on the board, out of order. Ask the children to help you rewrite them in order. Alternatively, prepare some large 0–10 number cards, mix them up and ask the children to put them into the correct order.
Five number sort Order random numbers from 1 to 30, five at a time.	Compare and order numbers, using the related vocabulary.	**Before:** Ask the children to compare two numbers (such as 17 and 14), order them and say the numbers between them. **After:** Play the game as a class. Choose five 0–30 numeral cards and ask the children to order them. Keep the pace sharp.

Name	Date

Count it away

◾ Count your toys as you put them away.

Dear Helper
This activity helps your child to count things accurately. Use it for counting up to ten items to begin with. Over time, extend this to counting up to 15 and then 20 items. Encourage your child to count by touching each item, moving it and saying the counting number. So if they are putting some toys back into a box, encourage them to pick up each toy in turn, say the counting number and put the toy into the box. Stop the count from time to time and ask: *How many have you counted? Look in the box and tell me. How many more are there still to count?*

Name	Date

Fishing

◼ Decide which fish to take out of the tank:

to total 3   to total 4   to total 5

to total 6   to total 7

◼ Write your sums here. The first one has been done for you.

2 + 1 = 3

Dear Helper
This activity helps your child to use addition skills when solving a problem. If they find it difficult, ask them to write a sum for each pair of numbers using the example to help you. Encourage your child to work mentally, starting with the larger number each time and adding the other number in ones. For example, to add 3 and 2, they could say: *three... four, five. So three add two is five.* When your child is confident with this, challenge them to make 6 and 7 by adding three numbers together.

PHOTOCOPIABLE ■SCHOLASTIC

Name	Date

Number search

- On the way home from school, look for five things with numbers between 0 and 20 on them.

- At home, draw a picture of where you found each number.

- Write the number on the picture.

Dear Helper

This activity helps your child to read and write the numbers from zero to 20. On the way home from school, talk with your child about the numbers that they see: car numbers, house numbers, prices in shop windows and so on. Encourage your child to read these numbers. Read aloud any larger numbers that they do not yet recognise. At home, encourage your child to draw what they have seen and write the numbers. If they find this difficult, encourage them to draw the number in the air first. Challenge your child to use the back of the sheet to write some larger numbers that they saw outside.

Name   Date

Star sums

- ◖ You will need two counters, pennies or buttons.

- ◖ Throw the counters onto the star. See what numbers they land on.

- ◖ Write a sum to add the two numbers together.

- ◖ Work out the total and write it down.

- ◖ Do this six times.

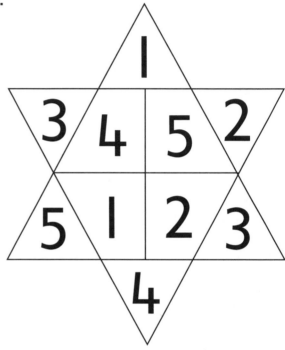

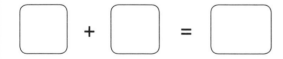

⬜ + ⬜ = ⬜   ⬜ + ⬜ = ⬜

⬜ + ⬜ = ⬜   ⬜ + ⬜ = ⬜

⬜ + ⬜ = ⬜   ⬜ + ⬜ = ⬜

Dear Helper
This activity will help your child to recall facts about addition with small numbers. If your child finds it difficult to recall the number facts, suggest to them: *Put the larger number in your head and count on in ones.* Discuss with your child how they worked out the answer to each sum. Challenge them to draw another star on the back of this sheet with the numbers zero to 10 in it, then try the activity again with the new star.

Name   Date

Number snap

- Cut out these cards.

- Shuffle them. Play 'Snap' with a partner.

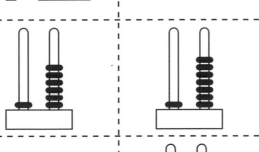

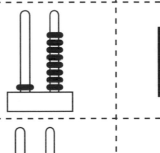

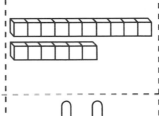

Dear Helper

This activity helps your child to recognise numbers from 10 to 20 that are shown in different ways. Play a game of 'Snap' by matching cards that show the same number (this may be a numeral or a pictorial image). If your child is uncertain, look carefully at the cards as they are turned over and ask your child either to read the number or to say how many tens and how many ones it has (for example, 15 has one ten and five ones). Challenge your child to play this game as quickly as possible: this will help them to read and count numbers quickly and accurately.

Name   Date

Creepy crawly add

◾ Count how many creepy crawlies there are in each box.

◾ Write the total in the box.

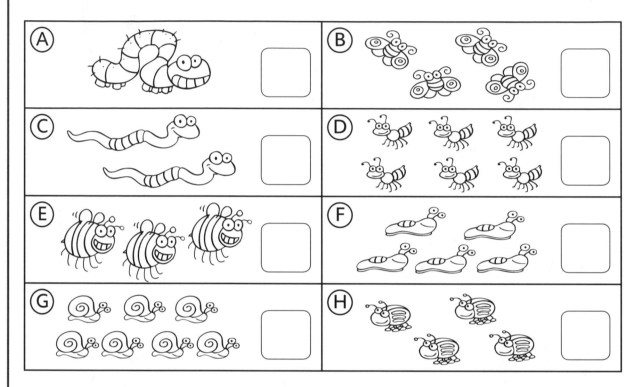

◾ Find two sets that make up a total of 8.

◾ Write the add sum in the boxes below.

◾ Find another three ways of making 8 from two of the sets.

☐ + ☐ = 8   ☐ + ☐ = 8

☐ + ☐ = 8   ☐ + ☐ = 8

Dear Helper
This activity helps your child to find different ways of making 8 by adding two numbers. Start by asking your child to count how many creepy crawlies are in each set, and to write that number in the box. Now ask them to choose one set and count on from that number by the number in another set. In the activity your child is looking for pairs that total 8. As an extra challenge, ask them to find three numbers that total 8, such as 1 + 2 + 5.

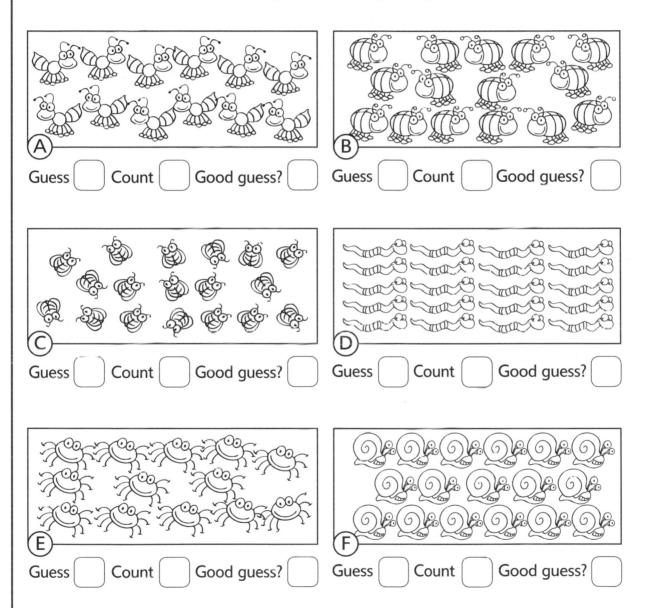

Name	Date

How many do you think?

- Look at these pictures of minibeasts. Do not count them yet.

- Guess how many there are in each picture. Write your guess.

- Now count them and write down how many there are.

- Put a tick in the last box if you made a good guess.

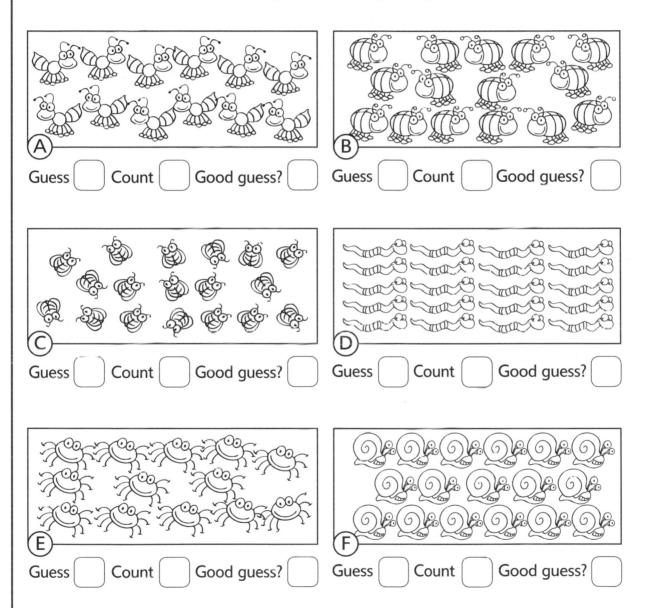

(A) Guess ☐ Count ☐ Good guess? ☐

(B) Guess ☐ Count ☐ Good guess? ☐

(C) Guess ☐ Count ☐ Good guess? ☐

(D) Guess ☐ Count ☐ Good guess? ☐

(E) Guess ☐ Count ☐ Good guess? ☐

(F) Guess ☐ Count ☐ Good guess? ☐

Dear Helper

This activity is designed to help your child estimate – that is, make a reasonably accurate guess. Look together at the first picture, and encourage your child to say roughly how many ants there are without counting them. Discuss how they worked this out, then ask your child to count. If your child finds the estimation difficult, put some pennies or counters into a spread-out pile and ask them to guess how many there are. Estimating skills improve with practice. Use everyday situations to get your child to estimate and then count – for example, how many chips or pasta shells on a plate.

Name   Date

Difference of 4

■ Find pairs of numbers with a difference of 4.

■ Write the numbers in these number sentences.

☐ – 4 = ☐

☐ – 4 = ☐

☐ – 4 = ☐

☐ – 4 = ☐

☐ – 4 = ☐

☐ – 4 = ☐

Dear Helper
This activity helps your child to understand the idea of subtraction as 'finding the difference' between two numbers. Encourage your child to start with a small number and count on, in ones, to add 4. For example: *three, then four, five, six, seven, so the difference between three and seven is four, so 7 – 4 = 3.* If your child finds this difficult, count on together and help your child to keep a tally of the count with their fingers. Challenge them to find larger differences, such as 5 or 6. The number sentences can be written on the back of this sheet.

Name	Date

A penny more, a penny less

You will need some penny coins.

Take a handful of pennies.

Write how many you have.

Now write what 1p more would be.

Now write what 1p less would be.

Do this five times.

I chose ⬜ pennies.   1p more is ⬜ p.   1p less is ⬜ p.

I chose ⬜ pennies.   1p more is ⬜ p.   1p less is ⬜ p.

I chose ⬜ pennies.   1p more is ⬜ p.   1p less is ⬜ p.

I chose ⬜ pennies.   1p more is ⬜ p.   1p less is ⬜ p.

I chose ⬜ pennies.   1p more is ⬜ p.   1p less is ⬜ p.

Dear Helper

This activity helps your child to decide what number is one more or less than a particular number. Start with a small handful of pennies. Ask your child to count them and then say what amounts are 1p more and 1p less. If your child finds this difficult, put the pennies in a line and count them together. Ask: *What is one more? What is one less?* Let your child count them again with one more, then one less pennies than the original count. Challenge your child to find 10p more and 10p less for handfuls of pennies between 10p and 20p.

Name	Date

More than 10

- Choose two numbers from the box to make a total of more than 10.

- Write the sum below. Do this five more times.

1 2 3 4 5 6 7 8 9

☐ + ☐ = ☐

☐ + ☐ = ☐

☐ + ☐ = ☐

☐ + ☐ = ☐

☐ + ☐ = ☐

☐ + ☐ = ☐

Dear Helper
This activity will help your child to use the strategy of bridging through 10 when adding two numbers. This means using their knowledge of the pairs of numbers (such as 6 + 4) that combine to make 10. So, for example, 6 + 7 is 6 + 4 + 3 = 10 + 3 = 13. If your child finds it difficult to see how to make the 10, provide a pile of counters, coins or buttons. Make a pile of 6 and a pile of 7, now take counters from the 7 pile to add to the 6 pile to make 10 (four counters), leaving a pile of 3. Now your child can work out 6 + 7 = 6 + 4 + 3 = 13 mentally, just writing the number sentence. Challenge your child to write some more addition number sentences that bridge 10.

Name	Date

Number order

- Play this game with a partner.

- Use all the playing cards ace to 10.

- Shuffle the cards. Place the pack face down on the table.

- Take five cards each.

- Place the cards in a line in front of you, face up.

- You now have to put your cards in order, from the lowest to the highest number.

- You are not allowed to move them around!

- Take turns to take another card from the pack.

- Decide whether to change it for one of your cards.

- If you do, put the card you have swapped at the bottom of the pack.

- Keep doing this until your cards are in order from lowest to highest.

- The first player whose cards are in order wins the game.

Dear Helper

This game helps your child to compare and order numbers. If your child finds the game difficult, ask them which numbers need to be changed. For each new card your child takes, ask where it could fit and which card could be thrown out. Challenge your child to play the game with six or seven cards to be ordered.

Name

Date

Five number sort

- You will need five counters or pennies.

- Throw the counters onto the number grid.

- Write your five numbers in order, from lowest to highest.

- Do this five more times.

- Write your numbers in the grid below.

- Remember to write them in order.

5	19	17	23	14
15	20	18	4	22
13	28	3	2	27
11	21	24	10	30
16	12	6	29	1

Dear Helper

This activity helps your child to compare numbers and put them in order. Encourage your child to use the counters to pick five numbers at random, and then to write them in order from the lowest number to the highest. If your child finds this difficult, ask them to decide which number is the lowest one, then to count from that number until they reach another of their numbers, and so on. When they have ordered all five numbers, count together from the lowest number to the highest and clap each time one of the five numbers is said. Repeat the activity five more times. Challenge your child to repeat the activity, this time ordering the numbers from the highest to the lowest.

Securing number facts, understanding shape

Activity	Learning objectives	Managing the homework
B1		
Coin sort Sort coins by their value, identify them and record by drawing around them.	Solve problems in the context of money.	**Before:** Look at 1p, 2p, 5p and 10p coins and check that the children recognise each coin. **After:** Review the homework together. Revisit coin recognition and values to give further practice if needed.
Coin totals Find different ways of making 8p. Write the sums.	Solve problems involving adding in the context of money.	**Before:** Explain that this activity will help the child to add up coins. **After:** Discuss the homework as a class. How did the children set about solving the problem? Ask individuals for their solutions.
Shape match Find examples of objects at home with the shapes of cubes, cuboids, spheres, cylinders and cones. Write the names of the objects in set rings.	Visualise and name common 3D solids.	**Before:** Explain that this activity will help the children to recognise 3D shapes in the world around them by their properties. **After:** Review the homework with the children. Make lists of objects found at home under their shape names, and put these up as part of a shape display.
Ice-cream cone Colour in six two-flavour cones, choosing from four flavours each time, to make each cone different.	Describe ways of solving puzzles and problems, explaining choices and decisions orally or using pictures.	**Before:** Discuss how each cone must be different from the others. Draw a white and pink cone and a pink and white cone on the board. Talk about how these are the same, so only one of them would count. **After:** Review the homework together.
Clown puzzle Colour in some faces, using three colours, so that each face is different.	Describe simple patterns and relationships; decide whether examples satisfy given conditions.	**Before:** Explain that this homework is a puzzle to solve. **After:** Using an A3 copy of the sheet, invite the children to demonstrate their solutions. Discuss how they solved the puzzle.
Steps of three Count items in threes to find how many are in each set.	• Count reliably at least 20 objects. • Read and write numerals from 0 to 20, then beyond.	**Before:** Practise counting from 0 to 30 in threes. Tell the children to count in threes, the items on the sheet. **After:** Review the sheet together. Count the items in each set in threes. Repeat, counting in ones, if children are unsure about this.
B2		
Shopping Choose from a selection of priced items within a total price of 10p.	Solve problems involving adding and subtracting in the context of money (for example, to 'pay' and 'give change').	**Before:** Suggest to the children that they may find using coins will help them to make their choices. **After:** Ask the children to select different choices of items. Discuss how they worked out the totals and the change.
2D shape search Search at home for items that have the same shapes as some common 2D shapes.	Visualise and name common 2D shapes.	**Before:** Ask the children to look around the room and name things that have a rectangular shape, then a square, triangular and circular shape. **After:** Ask individual children to name things from home that are square, triangular, rectangular or circular.
More and less With Helper, play a board game: say the number one or ten more or less than a given number.	Say the number that is one more or less than any given number and ten more or less for multiples of 10.	**Before:** Invite the children to say the numbers that are one or ten more or less than the numbers that you say. **After:** Discuss how knowing how to find the number one or ten more or less than a given number can help with adding or subtracting 1 or 10.

Securing number facts, understanding shape

Activity	Learning objectives	Managing the homework
Target tens Find different ways of making 10.	Derive and recall all pairs of numbers with a total of 10.	**Before:** Encourage the children to work methodically and not stop after finding just three or four answers. **After:** Play the call-and-response game with the class as described on the sheet.
Missing numbers Identify the missing number in a calculation.	Derive and recall all pairs of numbers with a total of 10 and addition facts for totals to at least 5; work out the corresponding subtraction facts.	**Before:** Show an example of a calculation with a missing number on the board. **After:** Challenge the class to find all the missing numbers.
Double trouble Learn doubles up to 10.	Recall the doubles of all numbers to at least 10.	**Before:** Talk about the word 'double' and make sure everyone knows what it means. **After:** Test the children's knowledge of 'doubles up to 10' with a quick-fire quiz.
B3		
Total 18 From a range of numbers provided, select pairs of numbers that total 18.	• Relate addition to counting on; recognise that addition can be done in any order; use practical and informal written methods to support the addition of a one-digit number to a one-digit or two-digit number. • Use the vocabulary related to addition and symbols to describe and record addition number sentences.	**Before:** Review the partitioning and recombining strategy for finding totals above 10. **After:** Invite children from each ability group to give an example of two numbers that total 18 and explain the mental strategy they used.
Symmetrical shapes Make symmetrical shapes by cutting out a box around each half shape, folding the box, then cutting around the half shape and unfolding.	Visualise shapes and use them to make patterns, pictures and models.	**Before:** Discuss the meaning of *symmetrical*. Demonstrate how to use a mirror to check whether a shape is symmetrical. **After:** Ask the children to say what each shape is after they have cut it out and opened it.
Shape search Match descriptions of 2D shapes to shape names. Find and draw things at home that have each shape.	Visualise and name common 2D shapes.	**Before:** Ask the children to describe a square, rectangle, triangle and circle. **After:** Ask children from each group to say which shapes and objects at home they matched to each description.
Twenty and more Play a game that involves adding two 'teens' numbers (without crossing the tens boundary).	Relate addition to counting on; recognise that addition can be done in any order; use practical and informal written methods to support the addition of a one-digit number or a multiple of 10 to a one-digit or two-digit number.	**Before:** Remind the children how they can use what they know to work out an unknown addition fact (for example: 3 + 5 = 8 so 13 + 15 = 28). **After:** Ask some of the questions from the sheet, so that the children work these out mentally. Encourage them to explain the mental strategies they used.
18p Find and record different ways of making 18p with coins.	Solve problems involving adding in the context of money.	**Before:** Discuss with the children how different coins can be used to pay the same amount. Use examples, such as different ways of paying 15p. **After:** Ask individual children to demonstrate with coins some of their ways of paying 18p.
Total 17 Find combinations of two numbers (chosen from a list) with a total of 17.	Solve problems involving adding in the context of numbers.	**Before:** Remind the children that it is possible to make a teens number by adding different pairs of numbers. Use examples, such as ways of making 14: 7 + 7, 6 + 8, and so on. **After:** Invite children from each ability group to give examples of how to make 17. Write these on the board. Encourage the children to explain the mental strategies they used.

BLOCK B

Name	Date

Coin sort

- ◀ Help Harvey sort his pocket money.

- ◀ Sort the coins by how much they are worth.

- ◀ Put them into the right purses.

- ◀ Draw round them.

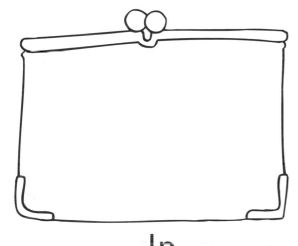

1p

2p

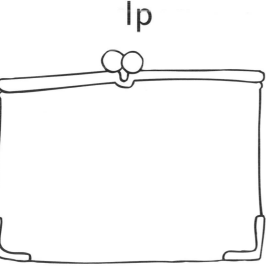

5p

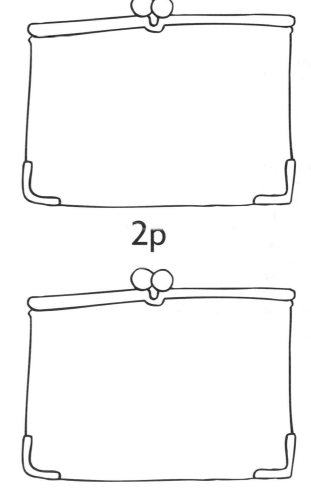

10p

Dear Helper

This activity helps your child to sort coins by value and name them. Put out a mixture of 1p, 2p, 5p and 10p coins. Ask your child to sort them by how much they are worth. Talk about the coins: their colour, the designs on both sides, and their value. Then ask your child to put the coins into the correct purses and draw round them. Encourage your child to record the design on the 'tails' side of each coin. Challenge them to sort other coins and draw these on the back of the sheet – you could provide 20p, 50p, £1 and £2 coins.

BLOCK B

Name	Date

Coin totals

- Gina has 8p in her purse.

- What coins could she have?

- Find four different ways to make 8p.

- Write a sum in each purse to show the way.

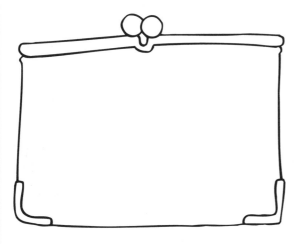
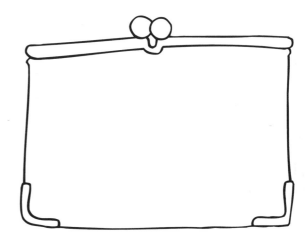

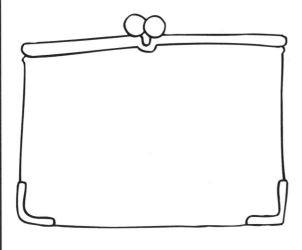
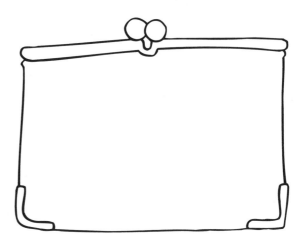

Dear Helper
This activity helps your child to add up coins. Put out some real 1p, 2p and 5p coins for your child to use in solving the problem. Check that they recognise the value of each coin. Suggest to your child that they add up coins to make 8p: *Put the larger number in your head and count on in ones.* In a combination where a 2p coin is being added on, check that they count on the 2p correctly (still in ones). Challenge your child to make larger totals (such as 13p) and record their work on the back of the sheet.

Name	Date

Shape match

◼ Look at home for things with these shapes.

◼ Write the name of each thing you find in the set ring for that shape.

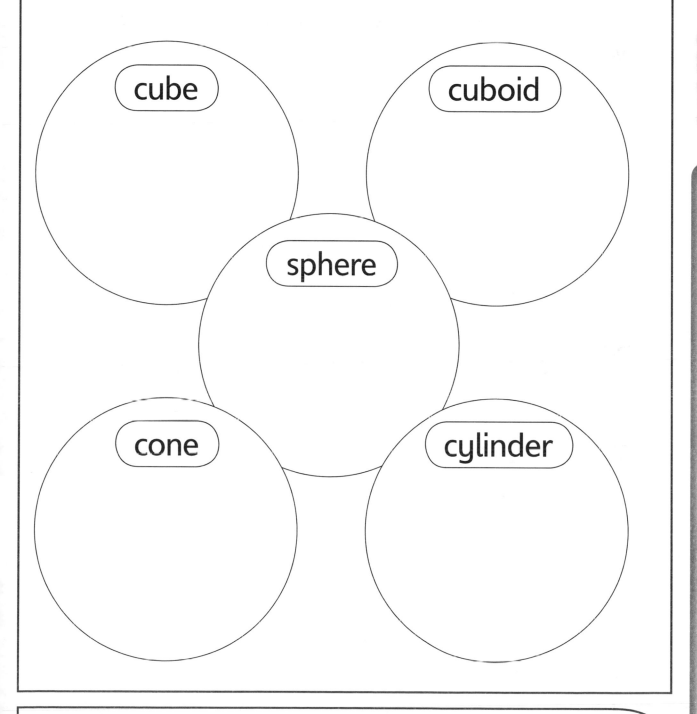

BLOCK B

Dear Helper
This activity helps your child to recognise some common 3D shapes. At home, work together to find items that are cubes, cuboids, spheres, cones or cylinders. Ask your child to explain why each chosen item belongs to a particular group. If your child finds writing the name of the object difficult, write it for them and encourage them to draw a picture of the object. Challenge your child to find other shapes, such as pyramids.

Name   Date

Ice-cream cone

● Percy has a double cone. It has two different flavours.

● Colour in the ice-cream tubs.

● Now choose two ice-cream flavours for each cone.

● Colour the ice cream in the cones to show the flavours.

● Make each cone different.

Chocolate   Orange   Vanilla   Strawberry

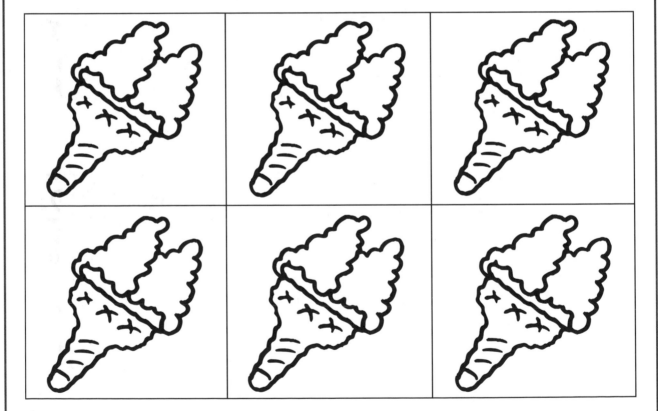

Dear Helper
This activity helps your child to develop problem-solving strategies. Ask your child to choose coloured crayons to show each of the ice-cream flavours. Each ice cream must be different. If your child finds this difficult, suggest that they start by colouring in the first cone chocolate and orange, then chocolate and vanilla, and so on. Talk about how chocolate and vanilla would be the same cone as vanilla and chocolate, just held the other way round. Challenge your child to draw some three-scoop ice-cream cones on the back of this sheet, then use them to show as many different combinations of ice-cream flavours as they can find.

PHOTOCOPIABLE ■SCHOLASTIC

Name   Date

Clown puzzle

■ Use only red, blue and yellow crayons or pencils.

■ Colour each clown's hat, scarf and hair using the three colours and making each clown different.

Dear Helper
This activity helps your child to develop logical thinking. Check that your child understands that for each clown, the hat, scarf and hair are to be coloured in differently, so that the red, blue and yellow crayons are used for each clown each time. If your child finds this difficult, complete the first clown together, deciding which clown feature will be red, blue or yellow. Discuss the next clown, deciding what will be different and what will remain the same.

BLOCK B

Name   Date

Steps of three

◼ Count in threes to find the total in each set.

◼ Write the totals in the boxes.

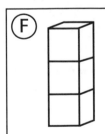
A

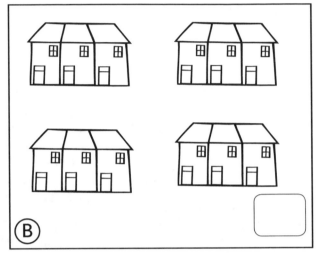
B

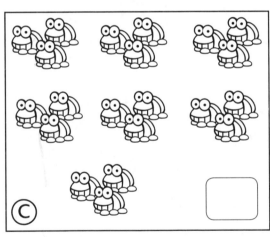
C

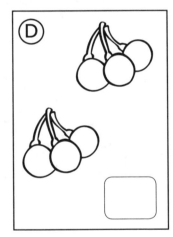
D

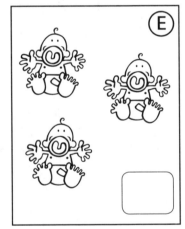
E

F

Dear Helper
This activity will help your child to count in threes. Before the activity, count together in threes from zero: zero, three, six, nine . . . up to about 30. Encourage your child to count the items in the pictures in groups of three. If they find this difficult, count each item together and stress the third one each time: one, two, **three**, four, five, **six**... Then count the items again, this time in threes. Challenge your child to draw some pictures of things in groups of three on the back of this sheet, and to write the total.

Name   Date

Shopping

- Pretend you have 10p to spend.

- Choose what you would like to buy.

1p

6p

4p

9p

2p

5p

3p

8p

7p

10p

- Will you have any change? [   ]   How much? [   ]

- Now buy some different things with 10p.

Dear Helper
This activity helps your child to use their problem-solving skills. Discuss with them which things they would like to buy. They may find it helpful to 'pay' you for the items with real coins, so that they can use the coins to work out the total and find the change. Challenge your child to make several different choices of items costing up to 10p, and then to make choices with a spending limit of 20p.

BLOCK B

Name	Date

2D shape search

◖ Look at these pictures.

◖ Find some things with the same shapes.

◖ Draw the things in the shape boxes.

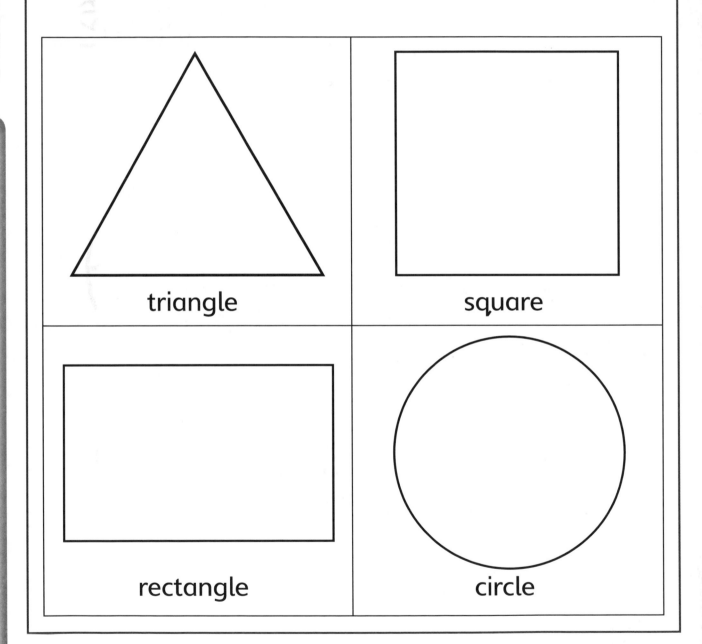

triangle

square

rectangle

circle

Dear Helper
This activity helps your child to recognise simple 2D shapes in everyday objects. Look together around the room. Find things that have a rectangular shape, such as a television screen, a window pane or a poster. Ask your child to draw these. Repeat this for the other shapes. If your child finds this difficult, ask them to run their hands over the shape object so that they can feel it is flat, even when the whole object is 3D. Challenge your child to find more unusual shapes around the house to record, such as star or crescent shapes.

BLOCK B

Name	Date

More and less

- Play this game with a partner.

- You will need a 1–6 dice and two counters.

- Put your counter on the Start square.

- Take turns to roll the dice.

- Move your counter the number of your dice score.

- Say the answer to the question on the square that you land on.

- Carry on until you reach the End square.

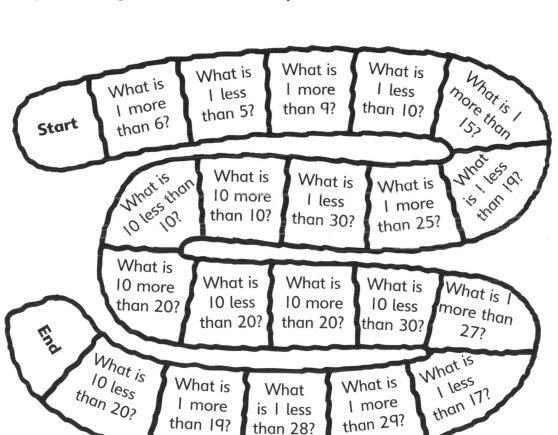

Start
What is 1 more than 6?
What is 1 less than 5?
What is 1 more than 9?
What is 1 less than 10?
What is 1 more than 15?

What is 10 less than 10?
What is 10 more than 10?
What is 1 less than 30?
What is 1 more than 25?
What is 1 less than 19?

What is 10 more than 20?
What is 10 less than 20?
What is 10 more than 20?
What is 10 less than 30?
What is 1 more than 27?

End
What is 10 less than 20?
What is 1 more than 19?
What is 1 less than 28?
What is 1 more than 29?
What is 1 less than 17?

Dear Helper

This game helps your child to recognise numbers that are 1 more or less, and 10 more or less, than any number. Play the game together. If your child finds it difficult to think of the answers, write out the numbers from zero to 30 in order along a line. Ask your child to find the number given, and then to find the number they are looking for by counting on or back by 1 or 10. Challenge your child to play this game quickly, so that they use rapid recall to find the answers.

BLOCK B

Name   Date

BLOCK B

Target tens

- You have two darts to throw at each target.

- You must score 10 each time.

- Both darts must score.

- Colour in two numbers that total 10.

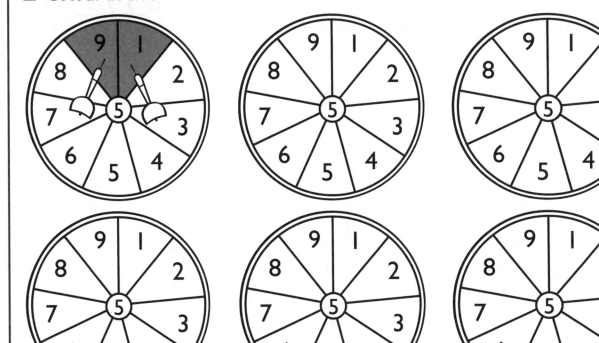

- How many ways are there to make 10 using pairs of numbers? Write them here:

_____

_____

_____

Dear Helper
This activity helps your child learn the number bonds to 10. This is essential groundwork for all forms of mental arithmetic; now and in the future. Practise them with your child until you're both confident they are learnt. You can play a quick-fire game with your child. You say a number between zero and 9 and they have to say the corresponding number to make 10. You can play this game any time and any where! Children love this one-on-one approach and it is a quick and easy way to cement the learning. As an extension, move on to number bonds to 20.

Name	Date

Missing numbers

◼ Freddy Fingers has taken some numbers!

◼ Help stop him and fill in the gaps.

1 + ☐ = 5

☐ + 3 = 5

4 + ☐ = 5

☐ + 5 = 5

10 – ☐ = 1

10 – 5 = ☐

10 – 7 = ☐

☐ – 8 = 2

10 – ☐ = 4

Dear Helper
This activity helps your child to learn addition and subtraction facts, which once embedded will never be forgotten! As with number bonds to 10, practice, practice dand more practice will enable them to be repeated without a second thought. Working out the missing number by looking at the calculation as a whole is another useful skill that is developed throughout the primary years.

Name   Date

Double trouble

◼ These are Class 1's sports day scores.

◼ Their teacher made a mistake!

◼ The scores should be double the number.

◼ Fill in the table with the new scores.

Name	Beanbag targets	New score
Ralph	7	
Leo	8	
Oliver	3	
Jessica	5	
Finley	9	
Enya	1	
James	4	
Kerry	2	
Lorcan	6	
Lihan	10	

Dear Helper
This activity helps your child to learn doubles, which is very useful for improving mental arithmetic.
When your child is confident with doubling numbers up to 10, extend the idea by doubling numbers up
to 20. Challenge your child by giving them speed tests!

Name	Date

Total 18

■ Choose two numbers from the pool that make a total of 18.

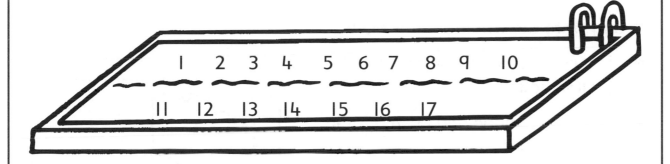

■ Write the addition sentence on one of the towels.

■ Do this another five times.

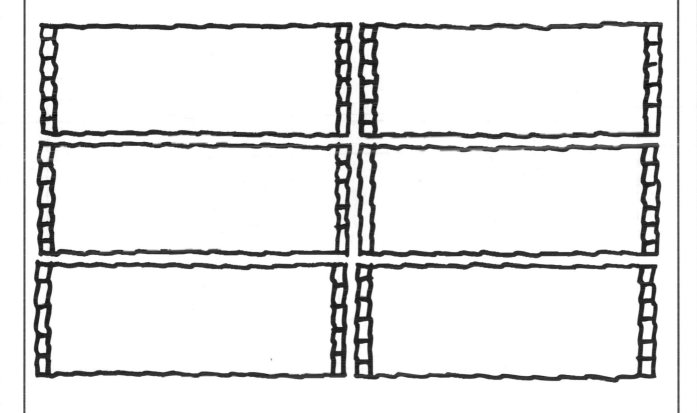

Dear Helper
This activity helps your child to use mental strategies for addition. Start by asking your child which two numbers they think will total 18. Encourage them to check their estimate by adding. Strategies that they could use include: partitioning and recombining (eg 8 + 7 = 8 + 2 + 5 = 10 + 5 = 15) and using facts already known (eg if 5 + 3 = 8 then 15 + 3 = 18). If your child finds this difficult, encourage them to count on in ones from the larger number. Challenge your child to find ten different solutions, using two or three numbers each time.

Name   Date

Symmetrical shapes

◼ You will need some scissors and a small mirror.

◼ Put the mirror on the fold line next to the first shape.

◼ Say what the whole picture will be.

◼ Now cut around the rectangle and fold it in half.

◼ Cut out the shape and open out the folded paper.

◼ Have you made the picture you expected?

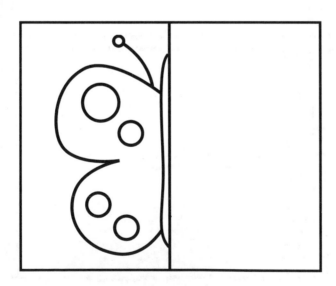

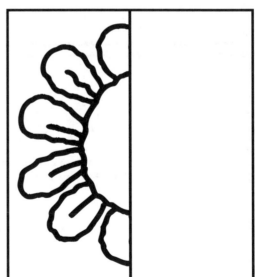

◼ Do the same thing for the other shapes.

Name	Date

Shape search

- Read these shape riddles.

- Draw a line to match each riddle to the correct shape.

- Draw some things from home that have the same shape.

I have 4 sides.
My sides are all
the same length.
What am I?

I am always round.
I have no straight sides.
What am I?

Rectangle   **Square**

Triangle   **Circle**

I have 2 pairs of sides
that are the same length.
My matching sides
are opposite.
What am I?

I have 3 sides.
All my sides are straight.
What am I?

Dear Helper

This activity helps your child to recognise familiar shapes from simple descriptions of them. Read the descriptions together and encourage your child to draw each shape from its description. If your child finds it hard to recognise the shapes, draw each shape next to its name and talk about the clues in the four descriptions to help your child match each shape to its description. Encourage your child to suggest some things that they could draw, such as a clock face for a circle, a television screen for a rectangle, and so on. Challenge your child to find three things at home for each shape.

BLOCK B

Name	Date

Twenty and more

● Play this game with a friend.

● You will need a 1–6 dice and two counters.

● Take turns to roll the dice.

● Move your counter the number of circles given by the dice.

● If you land on a circle with a question, work out the answer.

● The first player to reach 'Home' is the winner.

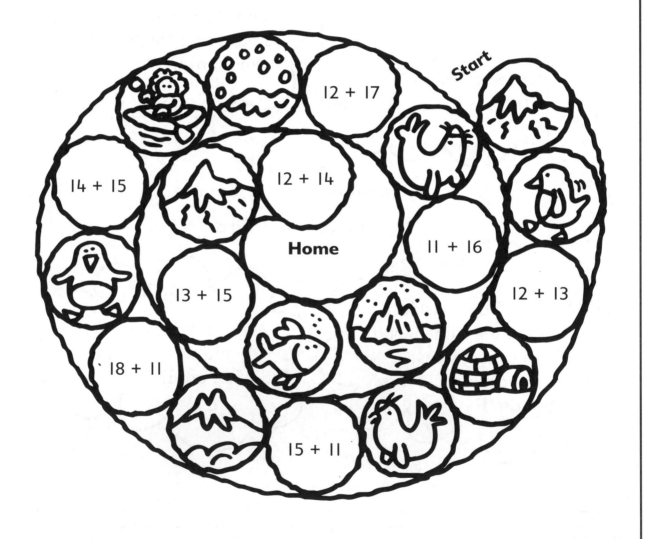

Dear Helper

This game helps your child to add two numbers between 10 and 20, using facts that they already know about adding numbers below 10. If your child finds this difficult, encourage them to look at the units. For example, if the question is 15 + 12, ask: *What is 5 + 2?* Play the game through several times, so that all the questions get answered. Challenge your child to work out the answers quickly.

| Name | Date |

18p

- You will need some coins.

- Choose some coins that make a total of 18p.

- Write an addition sentence to show which coins you have used.

- Find five more ways of making 18p. Record these.

- Tick the way that used the least number of coins.

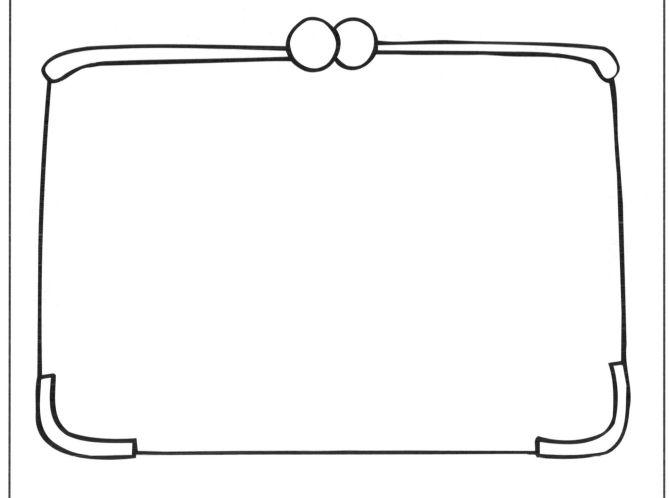

Dear Helper
This activity helps your child to use the mental addition strategies they have learned when using money. Your child will find using actual coins helpful for this. Encourage them to add up the coins they choose. If they find this difficult, ask: *What is this coin worth?* Then encourage them to count on from coin to coin. For example, if they have chosen 10p, 5p, 2p and 1p, they can say: *10p add 5p is 15p, and 2p more is 17p, and 1p more is 18p.* Challenge your child to find more ways of making 18p, and to write the extra solutions on the back of this sheet if necessary.

Name   Date

Total 17

■ Choose two numbers from the stars to make a total of 17.

■ Write the sum in the space below.

■ Do this another five times.

Dear Helper
This activity helps your child to use the mental addition strategies they have learned when solving problems. Ask them to start with two numbers that they estimate have a total of 17, then check by calculating. One way of doing this is to use a simpler number fact – for example, if 3 + 4 = 7 then 13 + 4 = 17. If your child finds this method difficult, suggest that they count on from the larger number they have chosen. Challenge your child to find ten solutions, adding two or three numbers each time.

Handling data and measures

Activity	Learning objectives	Managing the homework
C1		
Pencil length Estimate and compare the length of different items at home.	Estimate and compare objects using non-standard measuring instruments.	**Before:** Review how to compare two items for length. Remind the children that one end of both objects must be level. **After:** Discuss some of the items the children chose. Talk about how the estimate becomes more accurate with practice.
Comparing weights Find objects at home to compare for weight by holding.	Estimate and compare objects using non-standard measuring instruments.	**Before:** Remind the children how to compare two small objects for weight by holding one in each hand. **After:** Review the homework. Discuss which items the children found that were heavier/lighter than each other.
Favourite colours Complete a table of the favourite colours of family members and friends.	Answer a question by recording information in lists and tables.	**Before:** Explain that you would like the children to collect this information so that each group can use the data collected to make a chart back in school. **After:** Invite each group to create a chart showing favourite colours. Once the charts have been completed, ask questions such as: *Which colour do more/fewer people like, ___ or ___?*
Mug full Look for containers at home that hold about as much liquid (water) as a mug. Estimate which have the same capacity, then check.	Estimate and measure using suitable non-standard instruments.	**Before:** Ask the children to explain what an estimate is. Remind them that they need to estimate in order to find suitable containers. **After:** Invite some children to explain how they compared the capacities of their containers.
C2		
How many can you hold? Ask various family members or friends to take a full handful of crayons. Count the crayons. Record the counts on a chart and answer some simple questions.	Answer a question by recording information using block graphs.	**Before:** Review how to record in a chart by drawing simple pictures on squares. **After:** Invite some children to explain their results. Ask the class questions such as: *How many more/less crayons did ___ hold than ___? Who had most/least?*
How long is it? Estimate and then measure the length of some objects using uniform spoon lengths.	Estimate and measure objects using non-standard measuring instruments.	**Before:** Ask children from each group to demonstrate how to measure the length of an item using a set of identical spoons. Check that the children understand that the spoons must touch end to end. **After:** Discuss the children's results. Ask for explanations of why all the results are not the same. (Different sizes of spoons and items being measured.)
How many? Gather and record data from other family members; answer questions about the data.	Answer a question by recording information in lists and tables.	**Before:** Ask the children to help you compile a list showing their names and how many cubes they can hold. This can be written on the board. **After:** Discuss the data that the children have collected. These could be made into a whole-class chart. Ask questions such as: *How many ___? How many more ___?*
Colourful cars Use a pictogram to display data.	Use diagrams to sort objects into groups according to a given criterion.	**Before:** Discuss with the children what a survey is. **After:** Ask the children what they would like to do a survey on. Talk about any surveys they did at home with their Helper.
C3		
About a kilogram Make a kilogram weight, then find six things at home that children estimate weigh about the same.	Estimate and weigh objects using non-standard measuring instruments.	**Before:** Remind the children that an estimate is a 'good guess'. **After:** Test some things in the classroom that the children estimate weigh about a kilogram by balancing them against a one-litre bottle full of water on a balance.

Handling data and measures

Activity	Learning objectives	Managing the homework
Water fun Observe, discuss and record what happens when some coins are dropped into a small beaker of water.	Estimate and compare objects using non-standard measuring instruments.	**Before:** Discuss what happens to the bath water level when the children get into the bath at night. **After:** Invite children from each ability group to describe what happened to the water in the beaker as they dropped coins into it. They will probably realise that the coins have taken up some space in the beaker.
Favourite ice creams Use a pictogram to display data.	Answer a question by recording information in lists and tables; present outcomes using pictograms.	**Before:** Ask the children to explain how a pictogram is created. **After:** Go through the word problems on the worksheet with the class.
What's in the box? Sort objects into labelled boxes and draw extra objects.	Use diagrams to sort objects into groups according to a given criterion.	**Before:** Discuss with the class items that they have sorted such as pencils, books and so on. **After:** Ask for practical suggestions for classroom or bedroom storage. The children could then draw their ideas as a diagram.

SCHOLASTIC

Name	Date

Pencil length

◀ Find things about as long as your pencil.

◀ Find things shorter than your pencil.

◀ Find things longer than your pencil.

◀ Draw them here.

Shorter than my pencil	About the same length as my pencil	Longer than my pencil

Dear Helper

This activity helps your child to compare objects for length. Ask your child to find some small objects at home and decide (by estimating) which are about the same length as the pencil, longer than the pencil or shorter than the pencil. Then your child can compare them by placing each object next to the pencil. Check that your child matches one end of the pencil to one end of the object, so that they are level. This will help to make a more accurate comparison. Challenge your child to find something at home that is about as long as two pencils.

Name	Date

Comparing weights

- Choose some toys.

- Make sure you can hold each toy in one hand.

- Compare two toys. Decide which one is lighter.

- Draw them.

- Do this five times.

	is lighter than	
	is lighter than	
	is lighter than	
	is lighter than	
	is lighter than	

Dear Helper
This activity helps your child to compare objects by holding them and estimating which one is heavier. Encourage your child to find different sorts of toys to compare. If they find comparing difficult, ask them to hold one toy with both hands and then hold another toy in the same way. Discuss what they feel: *How heavy is each object?* Challenge your child to repeat this activity for some different objects, this time making the comparison *is heavier than...* They can draw more boxes and record on the back of this sheet.

PHOTOCOPIABLE **SCHOLASTIC**

Name	Date

Favourite colours

■ Who likes which colours?

■ Ask your family and friends.

■ Write their names by their favourite colours.

Favourite colour	Names
red	
orange	
yellow	
green	
blue	
purple	
brown	
black	

BLOCK C

Dear Helper
This activity helps your child to collect and record data. If your child finds it difficult to write down the names, help by writing these on the table. When all the names have been recorded, ask questions such as: *Which colour do the most people like?* Challenge your child to make their own table of fruit on the back of this sheet and collect some data about people's favourite fruit.

Name   Date

Mug full

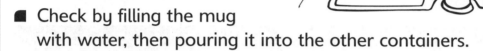

- You will need a mug.

- Find some other containers that you think hold about the same as the mug.

- Check by filling the mug with water, then pouring it into the other containers.

- Be careful! Do this over a sink or bowl.

- Draw your containers below.

BLOCK C

Holds less than the mug	Holds about the same as the mug	Holds more than the mug

Dear Helper

This activity helps your child to compare how much different containers hold. To avoid this becoming messy, your child could do this over a sink, washbasin or large bowl. If your child finds it difficult to estimate which containers will hold about the same as a mug, encourage them to make a collection of similar containers, such as cups, teapots and jugs. Your child can sort these containers by pouring water into each one from the mug. As your child pours water from the mug into another container, ask: *How full is this one?* Encourage them to use expressions such as 'half full' and 'nearly full'.

Name   Date

How many can you hold?

- Ask your family and friends to help. You will need some crayons.

- Pick up a handful of crayons.

- In one column, colour the boxes on the chart to show each crayon.

- Write your name underneath that column.

- Now ask three friends to pick up a handful of crayons.

- Each time, colour in the chart to show the crayons.

- Write each friend's name under their column in the chart.

How many crayons?			

Who held the most crayons? _____

Who held the least crayons? _____

Dear Helper
This activity helps your child to collect data, produce a chart, and answer questions about the data. Felt-tipped pens could be used instead of crayons. Encourage your child to carefully count the crayons they have picked up, then draw that number of crayons on the chart (one in each box in the column). Ask your child to write their name underneath. Repeat for three more people. When the chart is complete, read the two questions with your child. If your child finds answering these difficult, look together at the height of each column of the chart – this should help your child to see the answer. Ask questions such as: *Who held more/fewer than ___? How many more/fewer?*

BLOCK C

Name	Date

How long is it?

- You will need some spoons that are all the same length.

- Choose something at home that you could measure with the spoons.

- Estimate how many spoons long it is.

- Write your estimate in the table.

- Check by measuring and write your measure in the table.

- Now choose five more things to estimate and measure with the spoons.

What I chose to measure	My estimate	My measure
	spoons	spoons
	spoons	spoons
	spoons	spoons
	spoons	spoons
	spoons	spoons
	spoons	spoons

I am   at estimating and measuring.

Dear Helper
This activity helps your child to estimate and measure length. Your child will need a set of identical spoons for this activity. If they find measuring difficult, show them how to place the spoons end to end in a straight line. Things to measure could include, for example, the top of the television set, a cupboard top and across the bed. Challenge your child to use a different measuring unit, such as a set of forks, teaspoons or straws, to measure some of the chosen things again. Talk about why the results are different this time: the unit chosen is a different length from the original spoons.

Name	Date

How many?

- ◼ You will need some small building bricks.

- ◼ Ask your family and friends to help.

- ◼ Ask each person to pick up as many bricks as they can in one hand.

- ◼ Count the bricks and write the number in the chart.

Name	How many?

- ◼ Write the answers to these questions.

    1. Who picked up the most bricks?

    _____

    2. Who picked up the least bricks?

    _____

    3. Who do you think has the largest hands?

    _____

    4. Who do you think has the smallest hands?

    _____

BLOCK C

Dear Helper
This activity helps your child to count, and to record data. When your child has collected and recorded the data, ask questions such as: *Who picked up the most bricks? How many more bricks did ___ pick up than ___? How many fewer did ___ pick up than ___? How do you know that?* If your child finds this difficult, ask them to talk about which numbers on their chart are the largest and the smallest numbers. Challenge your child to work out the difference between the most and the least number of bricks picked up.

Name	Date

Colourful cars

◀ Pembe did a survey of the colours of cars going past her school in five minutes.

◀ She showed her data using a pictogram.

◀ Complete the pictogram by drawing the correct number of car symbols.

◀ The first one has been done for you.

Black cars: 6

Silver cars: 3

Red: 4

Blue: 5

Green: 2

Car colour	Number of cars with that colour
Black	🚗 🚗 🚗 🚗 🚗 🚗
Silver	
Red	
Blue	
Green	

Dear Helper

This activity helps your child to create a pictogram. You can do surveys at home by asking family members and friends about favourite foods or TV programmes. Your child can then be encouraged to present the findings as a pictogram. Pictograms are an introduction to handling data. Your child will progress to reading and using bar charts, line graphs, frequency tables and pie charts.

Name   Date

About a kilogram

- You will need a one-litre squash bottle.

- Fill the bottle with water and screw the top on tightly.

- The full bottle weighs about one kilogram.

- Now find some other things that weigh about one kilogram.

- Draw pictures of them.

Dear Helper
In this activity, your child will use estimation to choose things that weigh about one kilogram. Suitable things could include a standard bag of sugar or flour (cover up the weight information with a sticky label). Ask your child to hold the bottle and feel its weight. Now suggest that they compare this with different items from around the home. They should lift the bottle and the other item each time.
Ask: *Do they feel about the same weight?* Challenge your child to make a half-kilogram weight by filling a 500ml bottle with water, and use this to find things that weigh about 500 grams.

Name	Date

Water fun

- ◀ You will need a clear plastic beaker, a marker pen and some coins.

- ◀ Do this activity in the kitchen or bathroom.

- ◀ Make sure an adult is with you.

- ◀ Fill the beaker with water nearly to the top.

- ◀ Mark the water level with a marker pen.

- ◀ Now drop in coins one at a time.

- ◀ How many do you have to drop in to make the water come to the top of the beaker?

- ◀ Try this with different coins.

Dear Helper
This activity helps your child to understand that objects take up space (volume), and that we can use water to measure how much space they take up. Your child should enjoy this activity and not find it difficult. Your child may like to repeat the activity with a different beaker or coins. It can be linked to bath time – encourage your child to notice what happens to the water level when they get into the bath and get out again.

BLOCK C

Name	Date

Favourite ice creams

- This table shows the favourite ice-cream flavours of Sam's friends.

Strawberry	3
Vanilla	1
Chocolate	5
Coffee	2
Raspberry ripple	9
Toffee crunch	7

- Use this information to complete this pictogram.

- Use ⛄ as your symbol.

Strawberry	
Vanilla	
Chocolate	
Coffee	
Raspberry ripple	
Toffee crunch	

- Which is their favourite ice cream? _____

- How many children like strawberry and coffee altogether?

Dear Helper

This activity helps your child to become more confident at creating pictograms. Your child can begin to use the data in front of them to ask and answer questions relating to it. Try asking your child further questions about the data, such as: *How many more children liked chocolate than vanilla? What was the least favourite flavour? What was the total number of children who took part in the survey?*

BLOCK C

Name	Date

What's in the box?

- Luke is sending these things to the jumble sale.

- Which box should Luke put each item in?

- Draw a line from each item to the correct box.

Things to wear

Things to eat

Things to read

Things to play with

- Draw two more items in each box.

- Make sure they are in the correct boxes!

BLOCK C

Calculating, measuring and understanding shape

Activity	Learning objectives	Managing the homework
D1		
Making a cake Cut out pictures of events and arrange them in the correct sequence.	Use vocabulary related to time.	**Before:** Explain that this homework will help the children to become more confident in putting events into order of time. **After:** Review the homework as a class. Invite the children to tell the story that the pictures show.
Teapot full Estimate and measure the capacity of a teapot or saucepan, using some uniform non-standard units found at home.	Estimate and measure using non-standard units.	**Before:** Ask the children to suggest units that they could use at home to fill a teapot or saucepan with water. **After:** Invite some children to say which units they tried. Ask: *Were these good ones to use? Why?*
At what time? Join sentences that describe what a child is doing to clocks showing different times.	Read the time to the hour and half hour.	**Before:** Discuss with the children at what time they do things such as getting up and going to bed. **After:** Use the sentences on the sheet to stimulate discussion about the times at which the children do these things. The children can take turns to demonstrate the times they say, using the teaching clock.
Toy soldiers Estimate and count the number of toy soldiers.	Count reliably at least 20 objects, recognising that when rearranged the number of objects stays the same; estimate a number of objects that can be checked by counting.	**Before:** Count with the children up to 20 around the class. **After:** Play 'guess the amount of sweets in the jar'. Ask the class to count them with you. Small rewards optional!
D2		
Three coins Choose different sets of three coins, add them together and write sums.	Recognise that addition can be done in any order; use practical and informal written methods to support the addition of a one-digit number to a one-digit or two-digit number.	**Before:** Discuss strategies for finding totals, such as using addition facts already known, counting on or putting the larger number first. **After:** Invite some children to write a number sentence involving money calculations on the board for the others to attempt.
Sticker shop Choose things to buy from a list, and work out the change from 20p each time.	Solve problems involving adding or subtracting in the context of money (for example, to 'pay' and 'give change').	**Before:** Review finding change by counting up to 20p. **After:** Ask some children to give examples of what they chose and how they worked out the change.
Days of the week Children write about, and draw a picture to show, what makes each day of the week special to them.	Order days of the week.	**Before:** Review the order of the days of the week. **After:** Invite the children to talk about a special day in their week, such as the day of their dancing class, a special outing, and so on.
What is your hand worth? Children fill an outline drawing of their hand with 2p coins, then add up the amount of money.	Solve problems involving counting and adding in the context of money.	**Before:** Review how to add up 2p coins by counting in twos. **After:** Discuss how much the children's hands were 'worth'. Count in twos to the values of individual children's hands.
D3		
Inside the house Children draw furniture on a bedroom plan. They discuss where each item would be best placed, and why.	Visualise and use everyday language to describe the position of objects.	**Before:** Play a game of 'I spy', using positional language. For example: *I spy something on top of/under the cupboard; I spy something next to the table.* **After:** Ask some children where they placed the furniture on the floor plan, and to explain why they did so. Encourage them to use the language of position, direction and movement.

Calculating, measuring and understanding shape

Activity	Learning objectives	Managing the homework
Playing shops With Helper, choose two items from the sheet, add up the prices, then find the change from 20p.	Solve problems involving counting and adding in the context of money (for example, to 'pay' and 'give change').	**Before:** Review adding up the prices of two items (within 20p) and giving change from 20p. **After:** Ask the children to choose two items from the sheet, add the prices and work out the change. Discuss the mental strategies they used; how efficient were these?
Things that turn Discuss with Helper how the objects shown on the sheet turn.	Identify objects that turn about a point (eg scissors) or about a line (eg a door).	**Before:** Ask the children to stand up and demonstrate a whole turn, half turn, left turn and right turn. **After:** Review the sheet with the class. Discuss how each item turns.
Add and subtract Add and subtract amounts of money.	• Relate addition to counting on; use practical and informal written methods to support the addition of a one-digit number to a two-digit number. • Understand subtraction as 'take away' and find a 'difference' by counting up; use practical and informal written methods to support the subtraction of a one-digit number from a two-digit number.	**Before:** Review 10 + 2 and 10 − 2 with the children. Discuss how they worked out the answers. **After:** Review the sheet together. Ask children from each ability group to offer answers, and to explain how they worked them out.

| Name | Date |

Making a cake

- You will need: scissors, paper, glue.

- Cut out these pictures.

- Put them in the correct order.

- Stick them onto another sheet of paper to show how to make a cake.

Dear Helper
This activity will help your child to become more confident about ordering events in time. Before your child cuts out the pictures, talk about making a cake and what things need to be done. If they find the activity difficult, ask them to look at each picture, describe what is happening and then decide what comes next. Challenge your child to describe their day's events in the correct order. Prompt them with questions such as: *What did you do next? What happened before that?*

BLOCK D

Name   Date

Teapot full

◼ You will need a teapot.

◼ Choose some units to use, such as spoons, cups and egg cups.

◼ Estimate how many of each unit will fill the teapot.

◼ Check by filling the teapot with water, using your unit.

◼ Record how many units were used in the table below.

◼ Repeat this with different units.

I chose	My estimate	My measure
spoon		
cup		
eggcup		

I found the _____ the best unit to use.

It was the best because _____ .

Name   Date

At what time?

■ Read the sentences. Join each sentence to the time when it happens.

■ Sam gets up in the morning.   ■ Sam eats lunch.

■ Everyone eats breakfast.   ■ Sam walks home with Mum.

■ Sam gets to school.   ■ Sam helps to make the tea.

Dear Helper

This activity helps your child to read *o'clock* and *half past* times on a clock. It also helps your child to be aware of the times at which activities take place. Read each sentence together and look at the picture. Ask your child to decide what time it might be, then find a clock with this time. If your child finds this difficult, discuss where the hour and minute hands point to on the clocks and what times they show. Before your child draws lines to join the clocks and sentences, check that they have matched all of these. Challenge your child to think of some things that they do during the day, and at what times.

Name   Date

Toy soldiers

◢ Tom can't remember how many toy soldiers he has.

◢ Estimate how many soldiers Tom has.
  Remember, an estimate is a clever guess! _____

◢ Now count them. _____

◢ How close was your estimate? _____

BLOCK D

Dear Helper
This activity helps your child to estimate the number of objects. Young children enjoy estimating and counting so encourage your child at every opportunity. Developing your child's estimating and counting skills will hold them in good stead for their future maths learning.

Name	Date

Three coins

■ Choose three of these coins.

■ Make a sum. Write the total.

■ Make some different sums with the coins.

☐ p + ☐ p + ☐ p = ☐ p

☐ p + ☐ p + ☐ p = ☐ p

☐ p + ☐ p + ☐ p = ☐ p

☐ p + ☐ p + ☐ p = ☐ p

☐ p + ☐ p + ☐ p = ☐ p

☐ p + ☐ p + ☐ p = ☐ p

BLOCK D

Dear Helper
This activity helps your child to add up coins. Encourage your child to start with the largest number, then add the next largest number and so on. Help them to count on from the largest number, using their fingers to keep track. For example, for 5p + 2p + 2p: *5p add 2p is 5p... 6p, 7p; add 2p more is 7p... 8p, 9p.* Challenge your child to make ten different totals on the back of the sheet, and to include a 20p coin.

Coins © The Royal Mint

Name   Date

Sticker shop

◼ Choose a sport sticker to buy.

◼ Write the sport in the chart.

◼ Write how much the sticker cost.

◼ Work out the change from 20p.

◼ Write the change in the chart.

◼ Do this four more times.

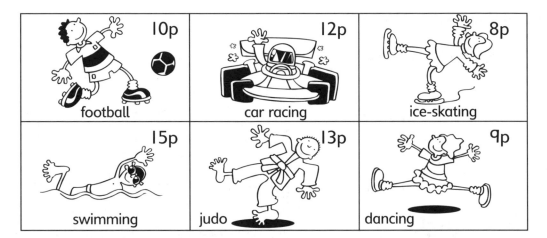

	10p football		12p car racing		8p ice-skating
	15p swimming		13p judo		9p dancing

I chose	It cost	Change from 20p

BLOCK D

Dear Helper
This activity is designed to help your child to work out the change from 20p for different prices. If your child finds this difficult, use real money: ask them to find the change by picking up coins. For example, for a price of 8p, 2p more makes 10p and 10p more makes 20p. So the change is 12p. Alternatively, your child could count up in pennies, then change these for the smallest possible number of coins. If your child has completed the activity, challenge them to find the change from 20p for two stickers.

Name	Date

Days of the week

- What do you do on each day of the week?

- Draw a picture for each day to show how it is special.

Sunday	Monday	Tuesday
Wednesday	Thursday	Friday
Saturday		

Dear Helper
This activity helps your child to remember the order of the days of the week. Talk about each day and what your child does that is special. It might be visiting grandparents on Sunday, going swimming on Thursday and so on. If your child finds it hard to identify the particular day on which something happens, help them by reminding them what happens on other days. For example: *What do you do on the day after swimming? Which day is that? And the day before swimming?*

Name   Date

What is your hand worth?

◪ You will need some 2p coins.

◪ Draw around your hand in the space. Fill your drawing with 2p coins.

◪ Now count up the coins.

◪ How much is your hand worth? Write the amount below.

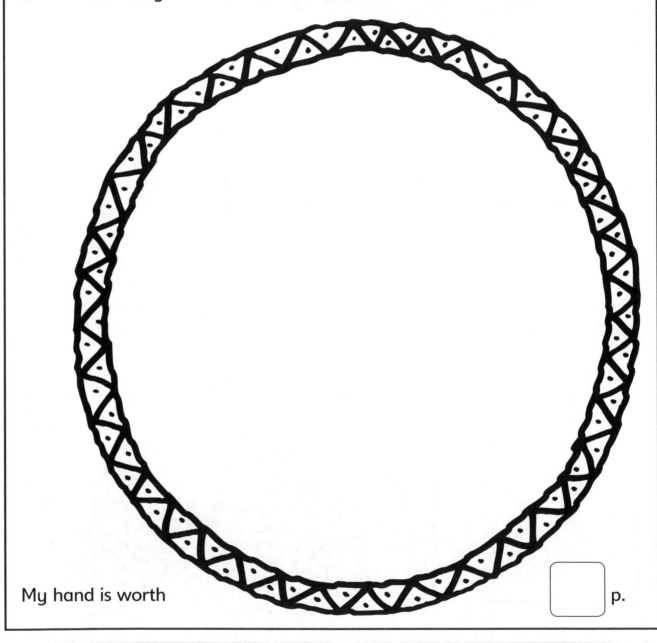

My hand is worth   ☐ p.

Dear Helper
This activity helps your child to add up coins, and to count in twos. It will be easier for your child to fill the outline of their hand with coins if they draw around their hand with the fingers closed. If your child finds counting the coins difficult, say together *two, four, six...* up to 30. Repeat this, asking your child to put the coins in a straight line and to touch each one as they count. Challenge your child to fill the hand space with a coin of another value and find out what their hand is worth now.

Name	Date

Inside the house

- ◣ You will need some coloured crayons.

- ◣ This is a drawing of a bedroom.

- ◣ It has no furniture in it.

- ◣ Decide where to put the furniture.

- ◣ Draw it there.

BLOCK D

Dear Helper

This activity will help your child to use words that describe position, direction and movement. Talk with your child about what furniture they would like in the bedroom, and where it should go. Encourage them to draw the furniture in place, and to explain why they have put it there using the language of position, direction and movement. If necessary, provide words such as *above, below, in, on, under, left* and *right*. Your child may want to use coloured crayons to make their picture more realistic. Challenge your child to choose another room in the house, draw it on the back of this sheet and then draw in the furniture. Again, ask your child to explain what is going where and why.

Name	Date

Playing shops

◀ You will need some coins and a friend to help you.

◀ Take turns to be the shopkeeper and the customer.

◀ The customer chooses two things to buy, to a total of 20p or less.

◀ The shopkeeper counts out the change from 20p.

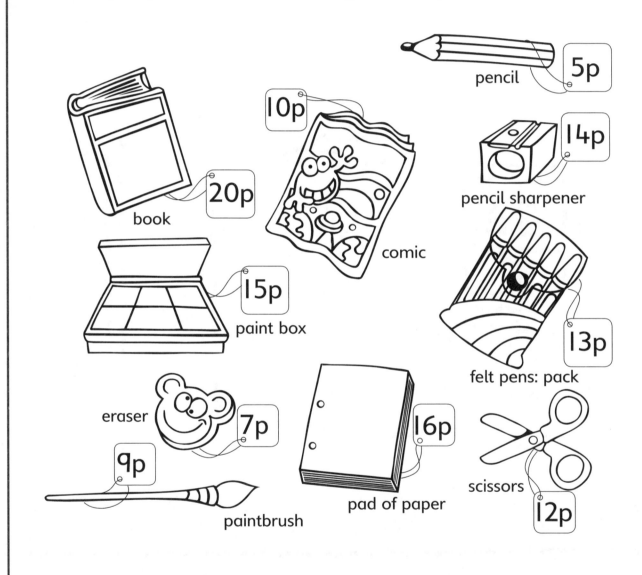

pencil **5p**

10p

14p

pencil sharpener

book **20p**

comic

paint box **15p**

13p

felt pens: pack

eraser **7p**

qp

16p

scissors

pad of paper

paintbrush

12p

Dear Helper
This activity helps your child to add up coins and to give change. Take turns to play the roles of shopkeeper and customer. Encourage your child to explain how they found the total price of the items they chose, and to give change by counting from the total up to 20p. If your child finds this difficult, use penny coins to count up from the total. For example, from a total of 17p: *1p is 18p, 1p more is 19p, 1p more is 20p. That makes 3p change.* When your child is confident with this, ask them to count on using higher value coins (for example, using 2p and 1p to make 3p). Challenge your child to choose three items and give change from 20p or 30p.

Name	Date

Things that turn

- Look at these pictures.

- Decide how the things will turn.

- Talk with your Helper about how the things turn.

Dear Helper

This activity helps your child to understand how different mechanical things can turn. Talk about each picture, and encourage your child to explain how the object turns. If they find this difficult, talk about whether it turns all the way round (like a spinning top) or turns by opening and shutting (like a pair of scissors). Challenge your child to find other mechanical things at home that turn, and to draw them on the back of this sheet.

BLOCK D

Name   Date

Add and subtract

(A)

■ How much does Marcia spend if she buys these pairs of items in the superstore?

■ Write the total for each sum.

  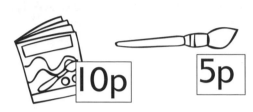

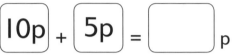

$10p + 3p = \boxed{}$ p $10p + 5p = \boxed{}$ p

 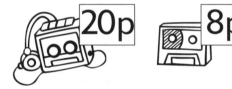

$20p + 4p = \boxed{}$ p $20p + 8p = \boxed{}$ p

(B)

■ Sean has 10p to spend.

■ What change will he have left if he buys one of these things?

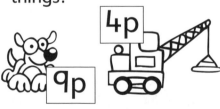

$10p - \boxed{} = \boxed{}$ p

(C)

■ You have 20p to spend.

■ What change will you have left if you buy one of these?

$20p - \boxed{} = \boxed{}$ p

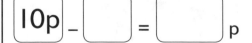

Dear Helper

This activity helps your child to add and subtract numbers to/from 10 or 20. If you add 10 or 20 to a number, the units digit of the number does not change (so 7 + 10 = 17). When subtracting a number from 10, your child should recognise that if (for example) 4 + 6 = 10 then 10 − 6 = 4 and 20 − 6 = 14. If your child finds this difficult, provide some coins to help them model the problems. They can use coins to add up the prices and to find change. Challenge them to solve these problems quickly and accurately.

BLOCK D

☐ Securing number facts, relationships and calculating

Activity	Learning objectives	Managing the homework
E1		
Missing numbers Fill in the gaps in some incomplete number sequences.	Count on or back in ones.	**Before:** Explain that this activity will help the children to be more confident about reading and writing numbers. **After:** Review the homework as a class, discussing how the children found the answers.
Count in tens Using 10p coins, count in tens.	Count on or back in tens.	**Before:** Show the children some 10p coins. Ask them to count how many pence there are altogether by counting in tens. **After:** Ask the children to count in tens from zero to 100 and back again. Repeat, starting at 20, 30... Count beyond 100 if the children are capable.
How heavy? Order objects according to their weight.	Describe a puzzle or problem using practical materials and diagrams; use these to solve the problem and set the solution in the original context.	**Before:** Give the children three objects to pick up and order from heaviest to lightest. **After:** Ask the children where they think items would appear in their list of objects.
Counting sheep Record calculations as number sentences.	Use the vocabulary related to addition and symbols to describe and record addition number sentences.	**Before:** Ensure that the children know what number sentences are. **After:** Ask the children to show you examples of number sentences in their work.
Double bubble Double numbers up to 10.	Recall the doubles of all numbers to at least 10.	**Before:** Make sure that all the children know what the word 'double' means. **After:** Use 'doubles' as part of your mental warm-up routine or as a five-minute filler.
Half-price sale Halve numbers and solve a halving word problem.	Use the vocabulary of halves in context.	**Before:** Make sure all the children know what the word 'halve' means. **After:** Ask the question *What is half of ___?* as a quick-fire quiz game.
E2		
Near doubles Choose adjacent numbers, and write their total.	Use the vocabulary related to addition and symbols to describe and record addition number sentences.	**Before:** Remind the children of the 'double add one' strategy using some examples as a class. For example, 3 + 4 is the same as 'double 3 add 1' or 'double 4 take away 1'. **After:** Mark the homework. Review the strategy with children who need help.
Monster numbers Continue some counting patterns in twos, threes and fives on number tracks.	Count on or back in twos and fives.	**Before:** Ask the class to count in twos, starting from zero, then 1. Ask: *Which numbers are odd/even?* **After:** Review the homework together. Invite some children to write the counting patterns on the board.
Counting pattern game With Helper, play a board game that encourages counting in twos, threes or fives.	Count on in twos and fives.	**Before:** Count together from zero to about 20 in twos, threes and then fives. Extend the activity beyond 20 if the children are capable. **After:** Use an A3 copy of the worksheet to play the game in class. The children can play in pairs for about ten minutes to practise these counting skills.
Odd and even sort With Helper, sort and order playing cards into lines of consecutive odd and even numbers.	Compare and order numbers using related vocabulary.	**Before:** Say together the odd numbers from 1 to at least 19, then the even numbers from zero to at least 20. **After:** Ask the children to explain how they knew which were odd numbers and which were even.

BLOCK E

Activity	Learning objectives	Managing the homework
At the sweet shop Count coins and answer word problems.	Solve problems involving adding or subtracting in the context of money (for example to 'pay' and 'give change').	**Before:** Make sure the children are familiar with 1p, 2p, 5p and 10p coins. **After:** Place a quantity of coins (total less than £1) in a jar. Ask the children to guess the total, then count it. Ask: *How much more do I need to make a pound?*
Alien invasion! Record methods of sharing groups of 2, 5 and 10.	Solve practical problems that involve combining groups of 2, 5 or 10.	**Before:** Use cubes or counters to practise sharing groups of 2, 5 and 10. **After:** Mark the homework and see who managed to save the Earth!
E3		
Difference of 2 Write number sentences to match the statement: *I can take one number away from another number and leave 2.*	Describe relationships involving numbers.	**Before:** Explain the homework to the children. Ask for one or two examples that fit the statement and write these on the board. **After:** Invite children from each ability group to suggest some subtraction sentences that fit the statement. Write these on the board.
Puzzled Pete Look for patterns to solve a puzzle.	Describe a puzzle or problem using numbers, and diagrams; use these to solve the problem and set the solution in the original context.	**Before:** Explain that the children may not get the answers straight away. **After:** Go through the answers and highlight successful methods used by the children.
Leaping frogs Use number lines to count on in twos, fives or tens.	Count on in ones, twos, fives and tens and use this knowledge to derive the multiples of 2, 5 and 10.	**Before:** Count in twos, fives and tens with the class. **After:** Have a 'multiples of 2, 5 and 10' quiz.
Football stickers Solve division word problems.	Solve practical problems that involve combining groups of 2, 5 or 10.	**Before:** Remind the children to read the questions carefully before answering. **After:** Mark the homework and go through the answers with the class.
Speed test! With Helper, test knowledge of doubles up to 10.	Recall the doubles of all numbers to at least 10.	**Before:** Tell the children that they will need someone to help them at home. **After:** See who had the fastest time and offer the opportunity to 'beat your record'.
Fishy fractions Identify halves and quarters.	Use the vocabulary of halves and quarters in context.	**Before:** Explain the words 'halves' and 'quarters' and show examples. **After:** Ask the children to show you examples of halves and quarters.

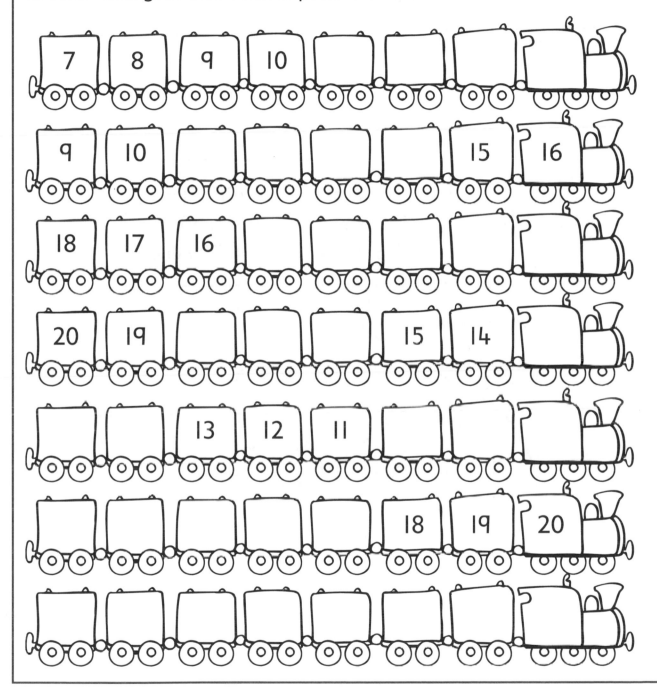
Name   Date

Missing numbers

◼ Write the missing numbers on these trains.

◼ Now write your own number pattern on the last train.

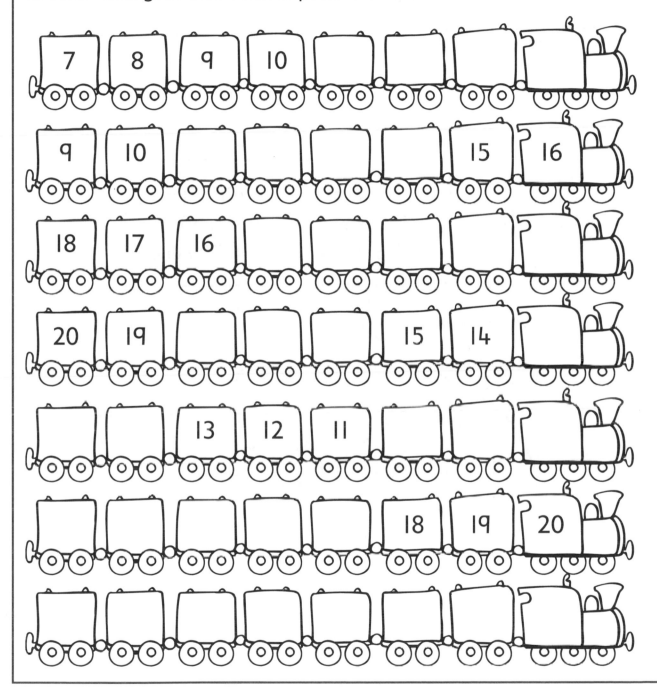

| 7 | 8 | 9 | 10 | | | | |

| 9 | 10 | | | | | 15 | 16 |

| 18 | 17 | 16 | | | | | |

| 20 | 19 | | | | 15 | 14 | |

| | | 13 | 12 | 11 | | | |

| | | | | | 18 | 19 | 20 |

| | | | | | | | |

Dear Helper
This activity helps your child to recognise the counting numbers in the correct order. Say the numbers on each train together, then discuss which numbers should go into the empty trucks. If your child is unsure which number comes before or after those given, say the counting numbers from zero to 20 and ask them to stop you when you say the required number. At the end of the sheet, there is a challenge where your child can write their own number pattern. A further challenge would be to ask your child to draw some more trucks on the back of the sheet and write numbers in these, including numbers above 20.

BLOCK E

Name   Date

Count in tens

- You will need some 10p coins.

- Take a handful of 10p coins.

- Count how many pence there are by counting the coins in tens.

There are five 10p coins.
I counted 10, 20, 30, 40, 50.
So these are worth 50 pence.

Dear Helper
This activity will help your child to count in tens. Practise counting in tens by saying the tens together, from zero to 100 and back again. Repeat this, using coins. If your child finds this difficult, explain that each coin is worth 10p – so by counting in tens, you can find out how many pence there are altogether. Your child may find it helpful to spread the coins out in a line, then count each one by touching it and saying the number. Challenge your child to count back from the total number of tens by touching the coins.

BLOCK E

Name	Date

How heavy?

- Here are some objects.
- Some are heavier than others
- The mountain is the heaviest!

- Order the rest of the objects, heaviest first.
- Write the number of the object in the correct box.

Heaviest	1								Lightest

BLOCK E

Dear Helper
This activity helps your child to order objects according to their weight. You could use a set of kitchen scales to measure the weight of various kitchen items. Set questions and puzzles for your child to answer. For example: *Which is heavier – three plastic beakers, a tin of beans or two wooden spoons?* Make predictions before testing and compare the results. Similar puzzles can be set using lengths of objects and measuring them with a ruler. Say: *Place these items in order of length, longest first.*

Name	Date

Counting sheep

◀ Write numbers in the sheep to make 12.

◀ Your answers are now number sentences.

◀ Farmer Lamb had 12 sheep. He bought three more sheep. How many sheep does he have now?

◀ Write your answer as a number sentence.

_____

Dear Helper
This activity helps your child to become familiar with the signs, symbols and vocabulary used in addition and subtraction. Use words and phrases such as *how many more, how many less* and *how many are there altogether* at home and help your child to say whether they need to add or subtract to work out the answer.

BLOCK E

Name   Date

Double bubble

- Bobby is forever blowing double bubbles!

- Write the double of these numbers in the empty bubbles.

BLOCK E

Name   Date

Half-price sale

- Generous George is cutting the price of his cakes on his cake stall.

- Each cake is now half price.

- Write the new cost of each cake in the cake boxes.

10p

16p

20p

40p

- Georgina sold a cake that was half the price of George's most expensive cake after he halved his prices. How much was Georgina's cake?

Dear Helper
This activity helps your child calculate halves. When out shopping, look at the prices of items with your child. Challenge them to find 'half price' stickers and labels. Maybe a small reward could be given for successful calculations!

Name   Date

Near doubles

■ Choose two next-door numbers from the box.

■ Write them in a sum and write the total.

■ The first one has been done for you.

$$1 \quad 2 \quad 3 \quad 4 \quad 5 \quad 6 \quad 7 \quad 8$$

1	+	2	=	3
+	=
+	=
+	=
+	=
+	=

BLOCK E

Dear Helper
This activity helps your child to use the 'double add 1' method for adding 'next-door' numbers. 'Next-door' numbers have a difference of 1 – for example, 1 and 2, or 5 and 6. Ask your child to say two next-door numbers, write them in the sum boxes, then find the total. If your child finds this difficult, remind them that they can double the smaller number and add 1. So, for example, 3 + 4 = 3 + 3 + 1. Challenge your child to write some more sums of next-door numbers on the back of this sheet, using larger numbers such as 9 and 10.

Name   Date

Monster numbers

- Continue these number patterns.

- Write the numbers that come next on the monsters.

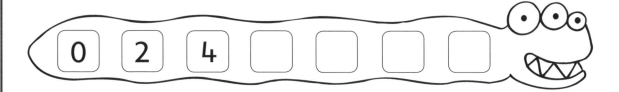

0 2 4 ☐ ☐ ☐ ☐

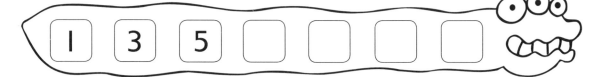

1 3 5 ☐ ☐ ☐ ☐

18 16 14 ☐ ☐ ☐ ☐

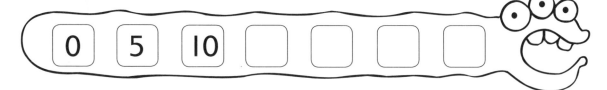

0 5 10 ☐ ☐ ☐ ☐

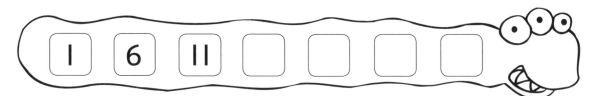

1 6 11 ☐ ☐ ☐ ☐

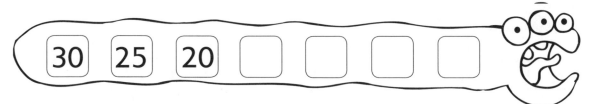

30 25 20 ☐ ☐ ☐ ☐

BLOCK E

Name	Date

Counting pattern game

- Throw a counter onto the circle. Will you move in steps of 2, 3 or 5?

- Cover a dice with six stickers and label each face 1, 2 or 3.

- Roll it to see how many steps to move.

- Count 2, 3 or 5 for each step as you move your counter.

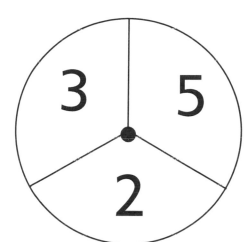

Dear Helper
This game helps your child to count in twos, threes and fives. Play the game together. If your child finds the counting sequences difficult, say them together. Play the game a number of times over a few days, until your child is confident with it. Challenge your child to count in twos using odd numbers.

BLOCK E

Name   Date

Odd and even sort

- ◖ You will need a set of playing cards without the picture cards.

- ◖ Play this game with a Helper.

- ◖ Shuffle the cards.

- ◖ Take turns to take a card.

- ◖ Say whether it is an odd number or an even number.

- ◖ Put the odd cards into a line in number order.

- ◖ Put the even cards into a line in number order.

Dear Helper
This game helps your child to recognise odd and even numbers. Play the game together several times, and encourage your child to play quickly. If your child finds it difficult to remember whether a number is odd or even, count together in twos from zero to 10, then from 1 to 9. This will help your child to see whether a particular number is odd or even. Challenge your child to write some more odd and even numbers from one to at least 20, in number order, on the back of this sheet.

Name   Date

At the sweet shop

◾ How much does each person have?

Beth has

Frankie has

Raj has

◾ Here are some sweets for sale.

◾ Which sweets could Beth buy? _____

◾ Raj buys a Chocco with one coin. How much change does he get?

◾ How many coins does Frankie need to use to buy a Fizz-bomb?

BLOCK E

Coins © The Royal Mint

Dear Helper
This activity helps your child to carry out calculations involving money. Adding up coins from moneyboxes and jam-jars is entertaining for most children, especially if they are going shopping! Handling coins is such a useful and natural way for children to learn about addition and subtraction.

Name	Date

Alien invasion!

- Captain Zap must save the Earth from an alien invasion!

- He has a keyboard with 20 buttons on it.

- Captain Zap needs to press the right groups of buttons to put up the deflector shields. He needs your help!

- Circle 10 groups of 2 buttons.

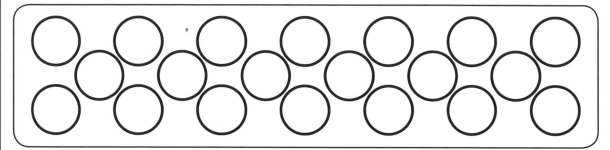

- Circle 4 groups of 5 buttons.

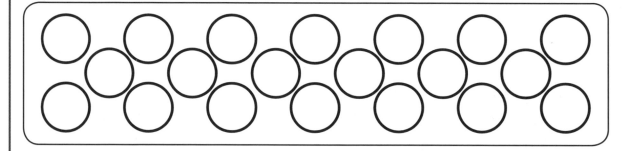

- Circle 2 groups of 10 buttons.

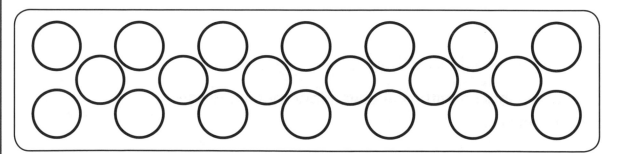

- If you've completed the task then the Earth is saved!

BLOCK E

Name   Date

Difference of 2

■ On the bears, write six subtraction sentences to match this sentence:
I can take one number away from another number and leave 2.

BLOCK E

Dear Helper

This activity helps your child to recognise that we can make general statements about numbers. Talk about pairs of numbers that have a difference of 2, such as 5 and 3, 8 and 6, 15 and 13, and so on. Ask your child to complete the number sentences on this sheet with their own suggestions. If they find this difficult, suggest that they think of a number, count on 2, then check whether the two numbers have a difference of 2. Challenge your child to write some more subtraction sentences for a difference of 2 on the back of this sheet. They may try some quite adventurous ones, such as 30 – 28 or 100 – 98.

Name   Date

Puzzled Pete

- Look for patterns to solve these problems and try different ways to make them work. There may be more than one correct answer.

- Puzzled Pete put the numbers 1, 2, 3 and 4 in the squares so that squares next to each other have a difference of more than 1. How did he do it?

- Puzzled Pete then put the numbers 1, 2 or 3 in the squares of this pattern so that each side of the triangle adds up to 5. How did he do it? (Each number can be used more than once.)

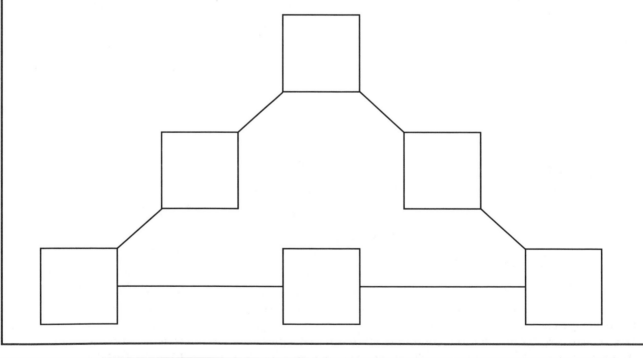

Name   Date

Leaping frogs

■ Freddie Frog starts from his rock and leaps in steps of 2.

What numbers does he land on? _____

① → ② → ③ → ④ → ⑤ → ⑥ → ⑦ → ⑧ → ⑨ → ⑩ → ⑪ → ⑫ → ⑬ → ⑭ → ⑮ → ⑯ → ⑰ → ⑱ → ⑲ → ⑳

■ Freda Frog starts from her rock and leaps in steps of 5.

What numbers does she land on? _____

① → ② → ③ → ④ → ⑤ → ⑥ → ⑦ → ⑧ → ⑨ → ⑩ → ⑪ → ⑫ → ⑬ → ⑭ → ⑮ → ⑯ → ⑰ → ⑱ → ⑲ → ⑳

■ Fergie Frog starts from his rock and leaps in steps of 10!

What numbers does he land on? _____

① → ② → ③ → ④ → ⑤ → ⑥ → ⑦ → ⑧ → ⑨ → ⑩ → ⑪ → ⑫ → ⑬ → ⑭ → ⑮ → ⑯ → ⑰ → ⑱ → ⑲ → ⑳

■ Which numbers do all three frogs land on? _____

Dear Helper

This activity helps your child to count on in steps of different sizes. Your child might find it helpful to draw the leaps on the number lines. If your child is comfortable with this activity, you could use the back of this sheet and extend the number line up to 100. In this way, your child could explore all the multiples of 2, 5 and 10 up to 100.

BLOCK E

Name	Date

Football stickers

◼ Wayne collects football stickers.

◼ He has 20 'swaps' to give to his friends.

◼ He wants to know how many stickers they will each get if he shares them between different numbers of friends.

◼ He shares the 20 swaps equally between two friends.
How many will they get each?

◼ He shares the 20 swaps equally between five friends.
How many will they get each?

◼ He shares the 20 swaps equally between ten friends.
How many will they get each?

Dear Helper
This activity helps your child to share things equally. 2, 5 and 10 are 'friendly' numbers that children should get used to working with. Being able to manipulate these numbers easily will greatly improve a child's mental arithmetic skills. It might help to use 20 stickers or playing cards for this activity.

Name	Date

Speed test!

◀ Double each of these numbers.

◀ Ask someone to time you.

◀ Write the answers as fast as you can.

1	→
8	→
6	→
4	→
9	→
2	→
7	→
10	→
3	→
5	→

◀ How have I done?

All correct in under 10 seconds = Gold medal

All correct in under 20 seconds = Silver medal

All correct in under 30 seconds = Bronze medal

Keep practising to get a gold medal!

Dear Helper
This activity helps your child to develop quick recall of number doubles. When your child is able to recall these doubles quickly and accurately, challenge them to learn the doubles of numbers to 20.

BLOCK E

Name   Date

Fishy fractions

◼ Look at this fish tank.

◼ Complete these sentences.

◼ Choose a word from the box to complete each sentence.

half	patterned	quarter

◼ One [   ] of the fish have stripes.

◼ One [   ] of the fish have spots.

◼ One quarter of the fish are [   ] .

◼ Colour half of the fish your favourite colour.

◼ Colour one quarter of the fish a different colour.

◼ Colour the other quarter of the fish another colour.

Dear Helper
This activity helps your child to use and understand the language of halves and quarters. Most children will grasp the concept of equal halves in everyday situations (particularly if asked to share a bar of chocolate, for example!). Quarters can be harder to understand but can be seen clearly if you are cutting an apple or slicing sandwiches into four.

Puzzles and problems: Objectives grid

The puzzles and problems activities can be used very flexibly to provide children with fun maths tasks to take home. The puzzles and problems are based on work that children will be covering during the year and should test their use and application of mathematics at an appropriate level. Where possible, children should be encouraged to try different approaches to solving these problems and to look for clues and patterns in mathematics.

The grid below lists each activity and identifies links to the different objectives within the Using and applying mathematics strand of the Renewed Framework.

	Solve problems involving counting, adding, subtracting, doubling or halving in the context of numbers, measures or money, for example to 'pay' and 'give change'	Describe a puzzle or problem using numbers, practical materials and diagrams; use these to solve the problem and set the solution in the original context	Answer a question by selecting and using suitable equipment, and sorting information, shapes or objects; display results using tables and pictures	Describe simple patterns and relationships involving numbers or shapes; decide whether examples satisfy given conditions	Describe ways of solving puzzles and problems, explaining choices and decisions orally or using pictures
1 Lollipops	✔				
2 Magic /	✔				
3 Box of frogs		✔			
4 More? Are you sure?	✔				
5 Hunt the rectangle		✔			✔
6 Let's play darts!	✔				
7 Mrs Spud	✔				
8 Shape up				✔	
9 Missing money	✔				✔
10 Looking in the mirror		✔			
11 Is that the time?			✔		
12 2D or not 2D?			✔		
13 So solid			✔		
14 Roll the dice	✔				✔
15 How old?	✔				
16 Homemade Jigsaw					✔
17 Toy shop	✔				
18 Double up	✔				
19 Halve it	✔				
20 Going bananas	✔				
21 Juggler	✔				
22 Multi-storey	✔				
23 Generous Jeanie		✔			
24 Measure up			✔		
25 Balancing act	✔				
26 Thirsty work!					✔
27 Coining it	✔	✔			
28 Safe cracker				✔	
29 Shady shapes				✔	
30 Mixed-up Mickey					✔
31 Guess the amount	✔				
32 Pairing-up challenge	✔				✔
33 Growbags	✔	✔			✔
34 Who am I?				✔	
35 How long?			✔		✔
36 My pet cat					✔

1 Lollipops

Jade bought a lollipop for 5p.

She paid for it exactly with coins.

Show the four ways she can do it.

1 _____

2 _____

3 _____

4 _____

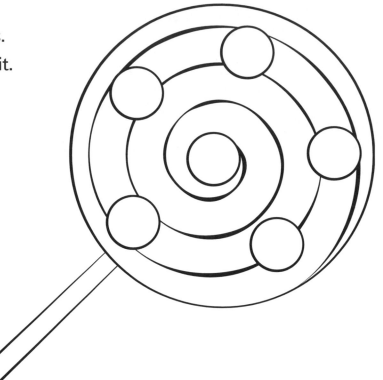

2 Magic 7

Make the number seven by adding the numbers on these cards.

How many ways can you do it?

| 1 | 2 | 3 |
| 4 | 5 | 6 |

3 Box of frogs

How many ways can you put the seven frogs in the three boxes?

Put your answers in the table.

One way has been done for you.

Box 1	Box 2	Box 3
I frog	2 frogs	4 frogs

4 More? Are you sure?

Dan has three more marbles than Stan.

Stan has two more marbles than Fran.

Fran has one marble.

How many marbles does Dan have?

How many marbles are there altogether?

5 Hunt the rectangle

How many rectangles can you find in this shape? Look carefully!

_____

6 Let's play darts!

Claire threw three darts.

Each dart hit the board.

More than one dart can go in each score.

What is the highest score Claire could get?

_____

Find some different scores that Claire could get.

_____

7 Mrs Spud

Mrs Spud has 10 potatoes and 5 hungry children.

Each child is given the same number of potatoes.

How many potatoes will they get each?

_____

8 Shape up

Draw the next two shapes in this sequence.

 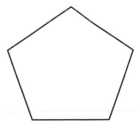  ? ?

9 Missing money

Forgetful Frank has lost one coin.

Which coin has he lost in these examples?

He should have 50p but only has two 20p coins.

Lost coin _____

He should have 70p but only has a 20p.

Lost coin _____

He should have 95p but only has a 5p, a 20p and a 50p.

Lost coin _____

10 Looking in the mirror

Draw circles round the four differences in the reflection of this drawing.

11 Is that the time?

I start school at 9 o'clock.

I am home by 4 o'clock.

I read at 6 o'clock.

I go to bed at 8 o'clock.

Draw the hands on the clock faces to show these times.

12 2D or not 2D?

2D shapes are flat shapes.

Draw a line from each name to the correct shape.

triangle   **quadrilateral**   **pentagon**

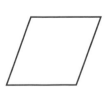

hexagon   **heptagon**   **octagon**

13 So solid

3D shapes are solid shapes.
Draw a line from each name
to the correct shape.

cone

cube

cuboid

cylinder

sphere

square-based pyramid

triangle-based pyramid

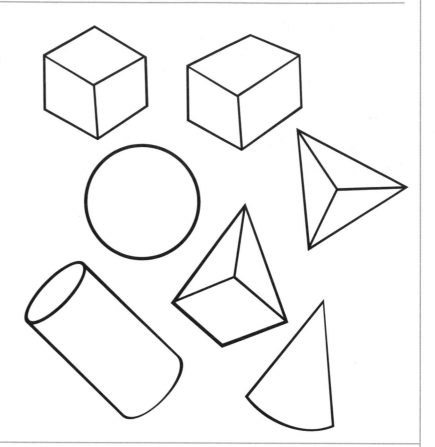

14 Roll the dice

Dan has two dice.
How many ways can
Dan score eight?

_____

15 How old?

Gertie is four years older than Bertie.

Bertie is 30.

How old is Gertie?

_____

16 Homemade jigsaw

Cut out an interesting picture from a magazine. (Ask first!)

Stick it onto a piece of card.

Cut it into 12 pieces.

Shuffle the pieces and put the picture back together again.

17 Toy shop

Roy has £10 to spend on
a toy.

He buys a toy car for £6.

How much does he have
left?

£ [ ]

18 Double up

Seniz has double the
amount of worms that
Ali has.

Ali has six worms.

How many worms does
Seniz have?

[ ]

19 Halve it

Ronny had 12 stickers and Jonny had 8 stickers.

They each gave Bonnie half of their collection.

How many stickers did Bonnie receive in total?

20 Going bananas

Charlie the cheeky chimp munched one banana then two bananas then three bananas.

How many bananas did Charlie munch altogether?

21 **Juggler**

Dizzy the juggler juggled eight eggs.

Dizzy slipped and dropped five of the eggs!

How many eggs did Dizzy have left?

22 **Multi-storey**

The multi-storey car park has three floors.

There are five cars parked on each floor.

How many cars are there in total?

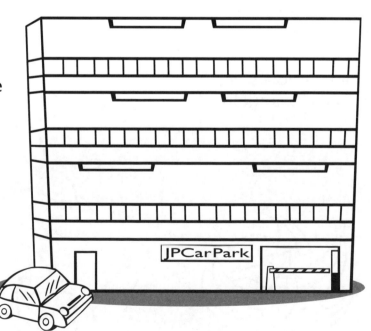

Puzzles and problems

23 Generous Jeanie

Generous Jeanie is sharing out some gobstoppers.

She has 18 gobstoppers to share equally between six friends.

How many gobstoppers does each friend get?

24 Measure up

Draw a line from each item to the correct unit of measurement.

Width of a book	litres
Weight of your teacher	metres
Length of a lorry 	kilograms
Capacity of the bath 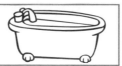	centimetres

25 Balancing act

Kim and Jim are standing on the scales together.

Eight bags of sand balance Kim and seven bags of sand balance Jim.

How many bags of sand are needed to balance them both?

26 Thirsty work!

After doing their homework Chantelle, Jack and Felix needed a drink.

They had a litre of lemonade in a jug.

How many millilitres of lemonade were left after they had all had a drink?

27 Coining it

Ros wanted to buy a bouncy ball that costs 30p.

She had three silver coins to pay for it.

Which coins could they be?

Find as many ways as you can.

28 Safe cracker

Freddie Fingers the safe-cracker needs to crack the code to open the safe.

What are the next three numbers he needs to fill in?

Write them in the boxes.

37, 38, 39

29 **Shady shapes**

Draw a circle round the shapes that are half shaded.

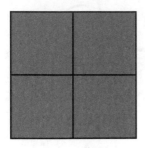 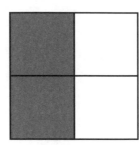 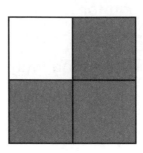

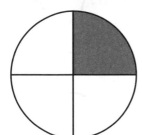 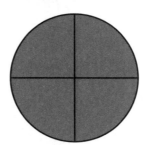 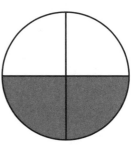

30 **Mixed-up Mickey**

Poor Mickey keeps forgetting how to write his numbers in words and in digits.

Help him with the correct answers.

Write 28 in words.

_____

_____

Write eighty-seven in digits.

_____

 100 MATHS HOMEWORK ACTIVITIES · YEAR 1

31 Guess the amount

An estimate is a good guess.

Estimate how many sweets are in this jar.

Write your estimate here.

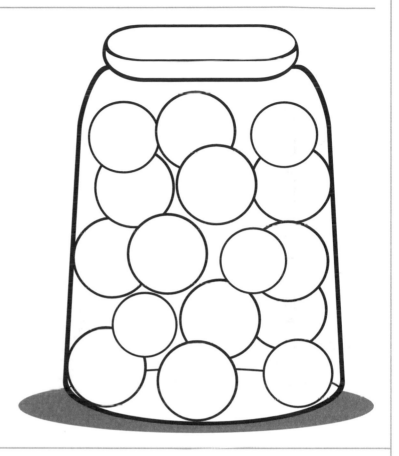

Now count the sweets.

There are ⬚ sweets.

How close was your estimate?

_____

32 Pairing-up challenge

Perfect Percy has found five ways to make 10 using two numbers.

He has challenged you to find more!

See if you can beat him.

Here is one to start you off:

9 + 1 = 10

_____

_____

_____

_____

33 Growbags

Talat has planted three flower seeds in each of these growbags.
How many plants will Talat grow in total?

34 Who am I?

I am a solid shape with just one face.

I am very useful in lots of sports!

What is my name?

_____

Can you draw me?

35 How long?

Number these wiggly worms in order from the shortest (1) to the longest (5).

36 My pet cat

Circle the instrument you would use to measure the weight of this cat.

On a separate sheet of paper, draw a toy that you might measure with a ruler.

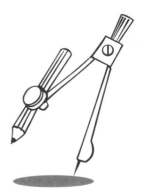

Homework answers

Block A

P9 Count it away No answers
P10 Fishing Answers will vary
P11 Number search Answers will vary
P12 Star sums Answers will vary
P13 Number snap No answers
P14 Creepy crawly add A: 1; B: 4; C: 2; D: 6; E: 3; F: 5;
     G: 7; H: 4; Answers in bottom section will vary
P15 How many do you think? A: 12; B: 15; C: 18;
     D: 20; E: 13; F: 17
P16 Difference of 4 Answers will vary
P17 A penny more, a penny less Answers will vary
P18 More than 10 Answers will vary
P19 Number order No answers
P20 Five number sort Answers will vary

Block B

P23 Coin sort Answers will vary
P24 Coin totals Answers will vary
P25 Shape match Answers will vary
P26 Ice-cream cone Answers will vary
P27 Clown puzzle Answers will vary
P28 Steps of three A: 18; B: 12; C: 21; D: 6;
     E: 3; F: 15
P29 Shopping Answers will vary
P30 2D shape search Answers will vary
P31 More and less No written answers
P32 Target tens 0+10; 1+9; 2+8; 3+7; 4+6; 5+5
P33 Missing numbers 4; 2; 1; 0; 9; 5; 3; 10; 6
P34 Double trouble 14; 16; 6; 10; 18; 2; 8; 4; 12; 20
P35 Total 18 Answers will vary
P36 Symmetrical shapes No answers
P37 Shape search

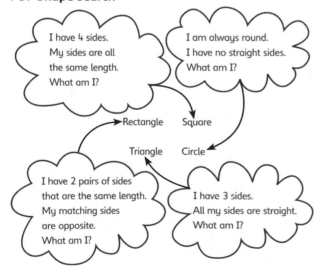

P38 Twenty and more No answers
P39 18p Answers will vary
P40 Total 17 Answers will vary

Block C

P43 Pencil length Answers will vary
P44 Comparing weights No answers
P45 Favourite colours Answers will vary
P46 Mug full Answers will vary
P47 How many can you hold? Answers will vary
P48 How long is it? Answers will vary
P49 How many? Answers will vary
P50 Colourful cars

Car colour	Number of cars with that colour
Black	🚗🚗🚗🚗🚗🚗
Silver	🚗🚗🚗
Red	🚗🚗🚗🚗
Blue	🚗🚗🚗🚗🚗
Green	🚗🚗

P51 About a kilogram Answers will vary
P52 Water fun Answers will vary
P53 Favourite ice creams Raspberry ripple; 5

Strawberry	🍦🍦🍦
Vanilla	🍦
Chocolate	🍦🍦🍦🍦
Coffee	🍦🍦
Raspberry ripple	🍦🍦🍦🍦🍦🍦🍦🍦
Toffee crunch	🍦🍦🍦🍦🍦

P54 What's in the box?

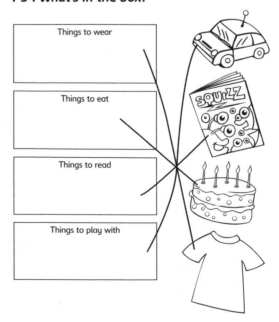

■SCHOLASTIC

Homework answers

Block D
P57 Making a cake B, D, A, F, E, C
P58 Teapot full Answers will vary
P59 At what time?

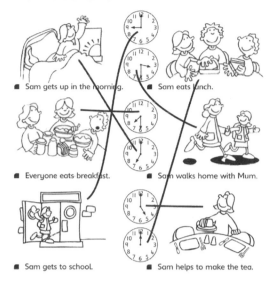

- Sam gets up in the morning.
- Sam eats lunch.
- Everyone eats breakfast.
- Sam walks home with Mum.
- Sam gets to school.
- Sam helps to make the tea.

P60 Toy soldiers 20
P61 Three coins Answers will vary
P62 Sticker shop Answers will vary
P63 Days of the week Answers will vary
P64 What is your hand worth? Answers will vary
P65 Inside the house Answers will vary
P66 Playing shops No written answers
P67 Things that turn No answers
P68 Add and subtract A:10p+3p=13p; 20p+4p
=24p; 10p+5p=15p; 20p+8p=28p;
B: 10p 9p=1p; 10p-4p-6p;
C: 20p-7p=13p; 20-5p=15p

Block E
P71 Missing numbers

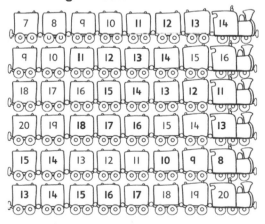

Last train: Answers will vary

P72 Count in tens Answers will vary
P73 How heavy? 1, 6, 3, 7, 4, 2, 8, 5
P74 Counting sheep Answers will vary, eg: 0+12;
1+11; 2+10; 3+9; 4+8; 5+7; 6+6; 12-0; 13-1;
14-2; 15-3; 15: 12+3 =15
P75 Double bubble 2; 6; 12; 14; 20; 22; 26; 30
P76 Half-price sale 5p; 8p; 10p; 20p; 10p
P77 Near doubles Answers will vary
P78 Monster numbers

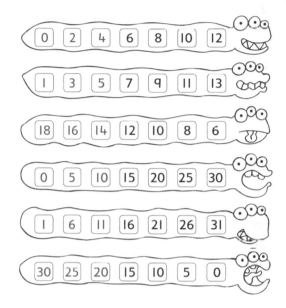

P79 Counting pattern game No answers
P80 Odd and even sort No answers
P81 At the sweet shop 7p; 11p; 13p; Chocco or
Chewchew; 3p; 4 coins
P82 Alien invasion! Answers will vary
P83 Difference of 2 Answers will vary
P84 Puzzled Pete 3, 1, 4, 2 or any combination
where consecutive numbers are not next to
each other; answers will vary for the triangle
pattern
P85 Leaping frogs 2, 4, 6, 8, 10, 12, 14, 16, 18, 20;
5, 10, 15, 20; 10, 20; 10 and 20
P86 Football stickers 10; 4; 2
P87 Speed test! 2, 16, 12, 8, 18, 4, 14, 20, 6, 10
P88 Fishy fractions half; quarter; patterned

Puzzles and problems answers

1 Lollipops 1p, 1p, 1p, 1p, 1p; 1p, 1p, 1p, 2p; 1p, 2p, 2p; 5p

2 Magic 7 Three ways: 1+6; 2+5; 3+4

3 Box of frogs 7, 0, 0; 6, 1, 0; 5, 2, 0; 5, 1, 1; 4, 3, 0; 4, 2, 1; 3, 3, 1; 3, 2, 2

4 More? Are you sure? Dan has six marbles; there are ten marbles altogether

5 Hunt the rectangle 18

6 Let's play darts! Highest score 12; other scores 3, 4, 5, 6, 7, 8, 9, 10, 11

7 Mrs Spud 2

8 Shape up Regular hexagon (six equal sides), regular heptagon (seven equal sides)

9 Missing money 10p; 50p; 20p

10 Looking in the mirror Logo on T-shirt; shoes; cap; mouth

11 Is that the time?

12 2D or not 2D?

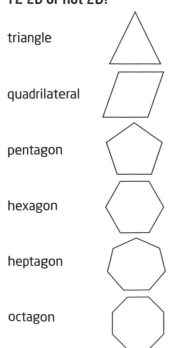

triangle

quadrilateral

pentagon

hexagon

heptagon

octagon

13 So solid

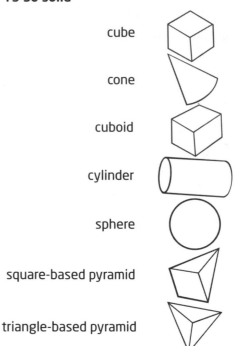

cube

cone

cuboid

cylinder

sphere

square-based pyramid

triangle-based pyramid

14 Roll the dice Three ways: 2+6; 3+5; 4+4

15 How old? 34 years old

16 Homemade jigsaw Child's own jigsaw

17 Toy shop £4

18 Double up 12

19 Halve it 10

20 Going bananas 6

21 Juggler 3

22 Multi-storey 15

23 Generous Jeanie 3

24 Measure up Width of a book - centimetres; weight of your teacher - kilograms; length of a lorry - metres; capacity of the bath - litres

25 Balancing act 15

26 Thirsty work! 500ml

27 Coining it 10p, 10p, 10p; 20p, 5p, 5p

28 Safe cracker 40, 41, 42

Puzzles and problems answers

29 Shady shapes

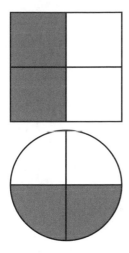

30 Mixed-up Mickey Twenty-eight; 87

31 Guess the amount 16 sweets

32 Pairing-up challenge 10+0; 9+1; 8+2; 7+3;
     6+4; 5+5

33 Growbags 18

34 Who am I? Sphere

35 How long?

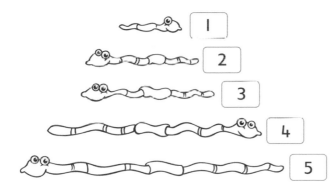

36 My pet cat Scales

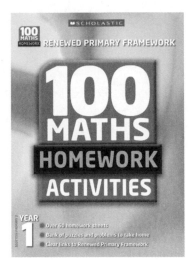
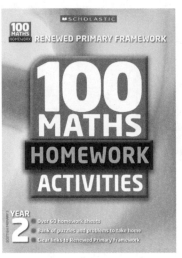
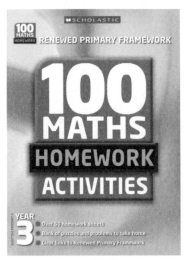
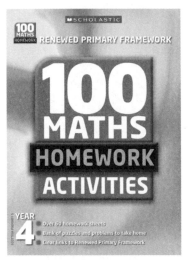

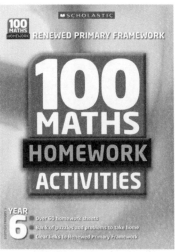